2017 SQA Past Papers with Answers

Higher
GEOGRAPHY

2015, 2016 & 2017 Exams

HODDER
GIBSON
AN HACHETTE UK COMPANY

This book contains the official 2015, 2016 and 2017 Exams for Higher Geography, with associated SQA-approved answers modified from the official marking instructions that accompany the paper.

In addition the book contains study skills advice. This advice has been specially commissioned by Hodder Gibson, and has been written by experienced senior teachers and examiners in line with the new Higher for CfE syllabus and assessment outlines. This is not SQA material but has been devised to provide further guidance for Higher examinations.

Hodder Gibson is grateful to the copyright holders, as credited on the final page of the Answer section, for permission to use their material. Every effort has been made to trace the copyright holders and to obtain their permission for the use of copyright material. Hodder Gibson will be happy to receive information allowing us to rectify any error or omission in future editions.

Hachette UK's policy is to use papers that are natural, renewable and recyclable products and made from wood grown in sustainable forests. The logging and manufacturing processes are expected to conform to the environmental regulations of the country of origin.

Orders: please contact Bookpoint Ltd, 130 Park Drive, Milton Park, Abingdon, Oxon OX14 4SE. Telephone: (44) 01235 827720. Fax: (44) 01235 400454. Lines are open 9.00–5.00, Monday to Saturday, with a 24-hour message answering service. Visit our website at www.hoddereducation.co.uk. Hodder Gibson can be contacted direct on: Tel: 0141 333 4650; Fax: 0141 404 8188; email: hoddergibson@hodder.co.uk

This collection first published in 2017 by
Hodder Gibson, an imprint of Hodder Education,
An Hachette UK Company
211 St Vincent Street
Glasgow G2 5QY

Typeset by Aptara, Inc.

Printed in the UK

A catalogue record for this title is available from the British Library

ISBN: 978-1-5104-2148-6

2 1

2018 2017

Introduction
Study Skills – what you need to know to pass exams!

Pause for thought
Many students might skip quickly through a page like this. After all, we all know how to revise. Do you really though?

Think about this:
"IF YOU ALWAYS DO WHAT YOU ALWAYS DO, YOU WILL ALWAYS GET WHAT YOU HAVE ALWAYS GOT."

Do you like the grades you get? Do you want to do better? If you get full marks in your assessment, then that's great! Change nothing! This section is just to help you get that little bit better than you already are.

There are two main parts to the advice on offer here. The first part highlights fairly obvious things but which are also very important. The second part makes suggestions about revision that you might not have thought about but which WILL help you.

Part 1
DOH! It's so obvious but …

Start revising in good time
Don't leave it until the last minute – this will make you panic.

Make a revision timetable that sets out work time AND play time.

Sleep and eat!
Obvious really, and very helpful. Avoid arguments or stressful things too – even games that wind you up. You need to be fit, awake and focused!

Know your place!
Make sure you know exactly **WHEN and WHERE** your exams are.

Know your enemy!
Make sure you know what to expect in the exam.

How is the paper structured?

How much time is there for each question?

What types of question are involved?

Which topics seem to come up time and time again?

Which topics are your strongest and which are your weakest?

Are all topics compulsory or are there choices?

Learn by DOING!
There is no substitute for past papers and practice papers – they are simply essential! Tackling this collection of papers and answers is exactly the right thing to be doing as your exams approach.

Part 2
People learn in different ways. Some like low light, some bright. Some like early morning, some like evening/night. Some prefer warm, some prefer cold. But everyone uses their BRAIN and the brain works when it is active. Passive learning – sitting gazing at notes – is the most INEFFICIENT way to learn anything. Below you will find tips and ideas for making your revision more effective and maybe even more enjoyable. What follows gets your brain active, and active learning works!

Activity 1 – Stop and review

Step 1
When you have done no more than 5 minutes of revision reading STOP!

Step 2
Write a heading in your own words which sums up the topic you have been revising.

Step 3
Write a summary of what you have revised in no more than two sentences. Don't fool yourself by saying, "I know it, but I cannot put it into words". That just means you don't know it well enough. If you cannot write your summary, revise that section again, knowing that you must write a summary at the end of it. Many of you will have notebooks full of blue/black ink writing. Many of the pages will not be especially attractive or memorable so try to liven them up a bit with colour as you are reviewing and rewriting. **This is a great memory aid, and memory is the most important thing.**

Activity 2 – Use technology!

Why should everything be written down? Have you thought about 'mental' maps, diagrams, cartoons and colour to help you learn? And rather than write down notes, why not record your revision material?

What about having a text message revision session with friends? Keep in touch with them to find out how and what they are revising and share ideas and questions.

Why not make a video diary where you tell the camera what you are doing, what you think you have learned and what you still have to do? No one has to see or hear it, but the process of having to organise your thoughts in a formal way to explain something is a very important learning practice.

Be sure to make use of electronic files. You could begin to summarise your class notes. Your typing might be slow, but it will get faster and the typed notes will be easier to read than the scribbles in your class notes. Try to add different fonts and colours to make your work stand out. You can easily Google relevant pictures, cartoons and diagrams which you can copy and paste to make your work more attractive and **MEMORABLE**.

Activity 3 – This is it. Do this and you will know lots!

Step 1

In this task you must be very honest with yourself! Find the SQA syllabus for your subject (www.sqa.org.uk). Look at how it is broken down into main topics called MANDATORY knowledge. That means stuff you MUST know.

Step 2

BEFORE you do ANY revision on this topic, write a list of everything that you already know about the subject. It might be quite a long list but you only need to write it once. It shows you all the information that is already in your long-term memory so you know what parts you do not need to revise!

Step 3

Pick a chapter or section from your book or revision notes. Choose a fairly large section or a whole chapter to get the most out of this activity.

With a buddy, use Skype, Facetime, Twitter or any other communication you have, to play the game 'If this is the answer, what is the question?'. For example, if you are revising Geography and the answer you provide is "meander", your buddy would have to make up a question like "What is the word that describes a feature of a river where it flows slowly and bends often from side to side?".

Make up 10 "answers" based on the content of the chapter or section you are using. Give this to your buddy to solve while you solve theirs.

Step 4

Construct a wordsearch of at least 10 × 10 squares. You can make it as big as you like but keep it realistic. Work together with a group of friends. Many apps allow you to make wordsearch puzzles online. The words and phrases can go in any direction and phrases can be split. Your puzzle must only contain facts linked to the topic you are revising. Your task is to find 10 bits of information to hide in your puzzle, but you must not repeat information that you used in Step 3. DO NOT show where the words are. Fill up empty squares with random letters. Remember to keep a note of where your answers are hidden but do not show your friends. When you have a complete puzzle, exchange it with a friend to solve each other's puzzle.

Step 5

Now make up 10 questions (not "answers" this time) based on the same chapter used in the previous two tasks. Again, you must find NEW information that you have not yet used. Now it's getting hard to find that new information! Again, give your questions to a friend to answer.

Step 6

As you have been doing the puzzles, your brain has been actively searching for new information. Now write a NEW LIST that contains only the new information you have discovered when doing the puzzles. Your new list is the one to look at repeatedly for short bursts over the next few days. Try to remember more and more of it without looking at it. After a few days, you should be able to add words from your second list to your first list as you increase the information in your long-term memory.

FINALLY! Be inspired...

Make a list of different revision ideas and beside each one write **THINGS I HAVE** tried, **THINGS I WILL** try and **THINGS I MIGHT** try. Don't be scared of trying something new.

And remember – "FAIL TO PREPARE AND PREPARE TO FAIL!"

Higher Geography

The Course

To gain the course award, candidates must pass the learning outcomes for all three units as well as the course assessment. The purpose of the course assessment is to assess added value of the course, confirm attainment and provide a grade.

The Exam

The course assessment is structured into Component 1, which is an externally set and marked question paper worth 60 marks, and Component 2, which is an assignment based on a research topic chosen by the candidate worth 30 marks. 90 marks are available in total.

Component 1 – The External Question Paper

The question paper is set and marked by SQA, and conducted in centres under exam conditions. Candidates are expected to complete this question paper in 2 hours and 15 minutes. The questions will be asked on a local, regional and global scale and the paper has four sections.

- **Section 1: Physical Environments – 15 marks**
  Candidates must answer all questions in this section.

- **Section 2: Human Environments –15 marks**
  Candidates must answer all questions in this section.

- **Section 3: Global Issues – 20 marks**
  Candidates must answer **two** questions from out of **five** options. Candidates must answer all parts of the question within each chosen option.

- **Section 4: A question on the application of Geographical Skills – 10 marks**
  This section consists of an extended response question requiring the learner to apply geographical skills acquired during the course. These may include interpreting an Ordnance Survey map, using six-figure grid references, understanding/using scale, direction and distance. You will also be required to extract and interpret information from a variety of sources. Candidates must answer this question.

The question paper component of the course assessment will have **a greater emphasis on the assessment of knowledge and understanding** than the assignment. The other marks will be awarded for the demonstration of skills.

Component 2 – The Assignment

The purpose of the assignment is to show challenge and application by demonstrating skills, knowledge and understanding within the context of a geographical topic or issue. Candidates can choose the topic or issue to be researched.

This assignment provides candidates with the opportunity to demonstrate higher-order cognitive skills and knowledge of methods and techniques.

- The assignment involves identifying a geographical topic or issue.
- It also involves carrying out research, which should include fieldwork where appropriate.
- Candidates will be asked to demonstrate knowledge of the suitability of the methods and/or reliability of the sources used.
- The assignment will involve drawing on detailed knowledge and understanding of the topic or issue.

- It will also involve analysing and processing information from a range of sources.
- It will require reaching a conclusion supported by a range of evidence on a geographical topic or issue.
- Candidates should demonstrate the skill of communicating information.

The assignment is set by centres within SQA guidelines, and the assessment is conducted under a high level of supervision and control by the presenting centre. The production of evidence for assessment will be conducted within 1 hour and 30 minutes and with the use of specified resources. This evidence is then submitted to SQA for external marking.

The assignment component of the course assessment will have **a greater emphasis on the assessment of skills** than the question paper.

Layout of this Book

This book contains three SQA exam papers. The layout, paper colour and question level are all similar to the actual exam that you will sit, so that you are familiar with what the exam paper will look like.

The answer section is at the back of the book. Each answer contains a worked-out answer or solution so that you can see how to arrive at the right answer. The answers also include practical tips on how to tackle certain types of questions, details of how marks are awarded and advice on just what the examiners will be looking for.

As well as your class notes and textbooks, these exam papers are a useful revision tool because they will help you to get used to answering exam-style questions. You may find as you work through the questions that they refer to a case study or an example that you haven't come across before. Don't worry! You should be able to transfer your knowledge of a topic or theme to a new example. The enhanced answer section at the back will demonstrate how to read and interpret the question to identify the topic being examined and how to apply your course knowledge in order to answer the question successfully.

Examination Hints

- Make sure that you have read the instructions in the question carefully and that you have avoided needless errors such as answering the wrong sections, failing to explain when asked to or perhaps omitting to refer to a named area or case study.

- If you are asked for a named country or city, make sure you include details of any case study you have covered.

- Avoid vague answers when asked for detail. For example, avoid vague terms such as "dry soils" or "fertile soils". Instead, try to provide more detailed information in your answer such as "deep and well-drained soils" or "rich in nutrients".

- If you are given data in the form of maps, diagrams and tables in the question, make sure you refer to this information in your answer to support any points of view that you give.

- Be guided by the number of marks for a question as to the length of your answer.
- Make sure that you leave yourself sufficient time to answer all of the questions.
- One technique which you might find helpful, especially when answering long questions, is to "brainstorm" possible points for your answer. You can write these down in a list at the start of your answer and cross them out as you go through them.
- If you have any time left in the exam, use it to go back over your answers to see if you can add anything to what you have written by way of additional text or including more examples or diagrams which you may have omitted.

Common Errors

Lack of sufficient detail

- This often occurs in Higher case study answers, especially in questions with high marks.
- Many candidates fail to provide sufficient detail in answers, often by omitting reference to specific examples, or by failing to elaborate or develop points made in their answer.
- Remember that you have to give more information in your answers to gain a mark.

Irrelevant answers

- You must read the question instructions carefully to avoid giving answers which are irrelevant.
- For example, if asked to explain and you simply describe you will not score marks. If asked for a named example and you do not provide one, you will forfeit marks.

Statement reversals

- Occasionally, questions involve opposites. For example, some answers would say "death rates are high in developing countries due to poor health care" and then go on to say "death rates are low in developed countries due to good health care". Avoid doing this. You are simply stating the reverse of the first statement.
- A better second statement might be that "high standards of hygiene, health and education in developed countries have helped to bring about low death rates".

Repetition

- You should be careful not to repeat points already made in your answer. These will not gain any further marks. You may feel that you have written a long answer, but it could contain the same basic information repeated over and over. Unfortunately, these statements will be recognised and ignored when your paper is marked.

Listing

- If you give a simple list of points rather than fuller statements in your answer, you may lose marks, for example, in a 5-mark question you will obtain only 1 mark for a list.

Bullet points

- The same rule applies to a simple list of bullet points. However, if you give bullet points with some detailed explanation, you could achieve full marks.

Types of Questions and Command Words

In these past papers, and in the exam itself, a number of command words will be used in the different types of questions you will encounter. The command words are used to show you how you should answer a question; some words indicate that you should write more than others. If you familiarise yourself with these command words, it will help you to structure your answers more effectively. The question types to look out for are listed below.

Explain

These questions ask you to explain and give reasons, for example, "strategies" and relationships. If resources are provided in the question, make sure you refer to them in your answer. Some marks may be allowed for description but these will be quite restricted.

Analyse

This involves identifying parts and the relationships between them by showing the links between different components and related concepts, noting similarities and differences, explaining possible consequences and implications, and explaining the impact of, for example, processes of degradation, strategies adopted to control events and government policies on people and the environment.

Evaluate

This will involve making judgements on, for example, the relative success or failure of strategies and projects such as a river basin management scheme or aid programmes.

Discuss

These questions ask you to develop your thoughts, for example, on a specific project or change in specified situations. You may be asked to consider both sides of an argument and provide a range of comments on each viewpoint.

Geographical Skills

This question is designed to examine your geographical skills. You will be given an Ordnance Survey map along with a variety of other resources which might include a climate graph, information table, newspaper article, statistics and photographs. You will be given a set of conditions to follow; these should be used to help you answer the question. You should use/evaluate the information you have been given to make judgements and back up your answer with map evidence, information from the diagrams and tables, etc. Remember the diagrams and OS map are there for a purpose and contain valuable information that you should incorporate in your answer!

Good luck!

Remember that the rewards for passing Higher Geography are well worth it! Your pass will help you get the future you want for yourself. In the exam, be confident in your own ability. Watch your time and pace yourself carefully. If you're not sure how to answer a question, trust your instincts and just give it a go anyway – keep calm and don't panic! GOOD LUCK!

HIGHER

2015

National Qualifications 2015

X733/76/11

Geography

THURSDAY, 21 MAY

9:00 AM – 11:15 AM

Total marks — 60

SECTION 1 — PHYSICAL ENVIRONMENTS — 15 marks

Attempt ALL questions.

SECTION 2 — HUMAN ENVIRONMENTS — 15 marks

Attempt ALL questions.

SECTION 3 — GLOBAL ISSUES — 20 marks

Attempt TWO questions.

SECTION 4 — APPLICATION OF GEOGRAPHICAL SKILLS — 10 marks

Attempt the question.

Credit will be given for appropriately labelled sketch maps and diagrams.

Write your answers clearly in the answer booklet provided. In the answer booklet you must clearly identify the question number you are attempting.

Use **blue** or **black** ink.

Before leaving the examination room you must give your answer booklet to the Invigilator; if you do not you may lose all the marks for this paper.

MARKS

SECTION 1: PHYSICAL ENVIRONMENTS – 15 marks
Attempt ALL questions

Question 1

Study Diagram Q1 before answering this question.

Diagram Q1: Flood Hydrograph for the River Valency at Boscastle, 16 August 2004

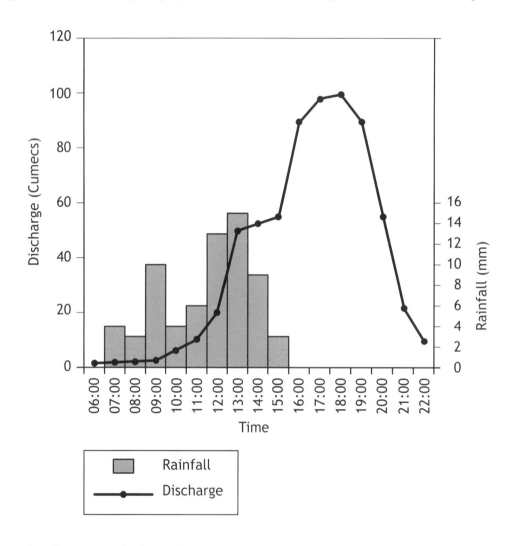

Explain the changes in discharge level of the River Valency at Boscastle on 16 August 2004.   4

MARKS

Question 2

Explain, with the aid of annotated diagrams, the various stages and processes involved in the formation of:

(a)   a stack; **and**

(b)   a sand spit.   7

[Turn over

your doing great sweety
keep up the good work
xoxo

Question 3

Look at Diagram Q3 before answering this question.

Diagram Q3: Surface winds and pressure zones

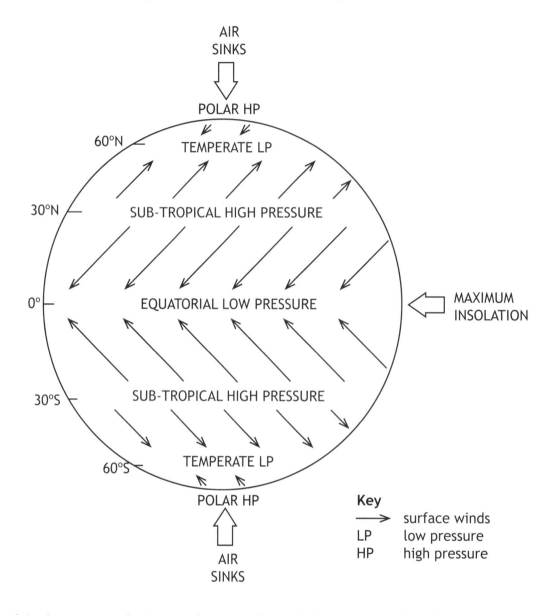

Explain how atmospheric circulation cells and the associated surface winds assist in redistributing energy around the world.

4

SECTION 2: HUMAN ENVIRONMENTS – 15 marks

Attempt ALL questions

MARKS

Question 4

Study Diagrams Q4A and Q4B before answering this question.

Diagram Q4A: Population Pyramid for Ghana, 2013

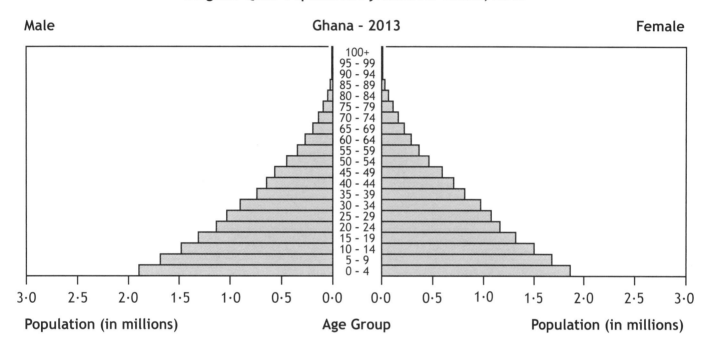

Diagram Q4B: Population Pyramid for Ghana, 2050 (predicted)

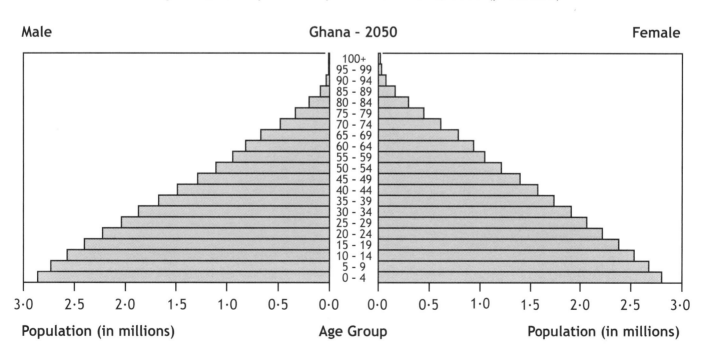

Discuss the possible consequences for Ghana of the 2050 population structure.

5

Question 5

Look at Diagram Q5 before answering this question.

Traffic congestion is a major problem in cities in the UK and across the **developed** world.

Diagram Q5: Most congested UK cities, 2013

Rank	City	Congestion trend
1	Belfast	Up
2	Bristol	Level
3	Brighton	Up
4	Edinburgh	Down
5	London	Up
6	Leeds/Bradford	Down
7	Manchester	Up
8	Leicester	Up
9	Sheffield	Up
10	Liverpool	Up

Explain the strategies employed to combat the problems of traffic congestion in a **developed** world city you have studied. You should refer to specific named examples from your chosen city.

5

MARKS

Question 6

Look at Diagram Q6 before answering this question.

Rapid urbanisation in **developing** world cities has resulted in many housing problems.

Diagram Q6: Photograph of Dharavi Slum, Mumbai, India

Evaluate the impact of strategies employed to manage housing problems in a **developing** world city you have studied.

5

[Turn over

SECTION 3: GLOBAL ISSUES - 20 marks
Attempt TWO questions

MARKS

Question 7: River Basin Management

(a) **Explain** the human **and** physical factors which need to be considered when selecting a site for a major dam and its associated reservoir.

5

(b) Referring to a water control project you have studied, **explain** the **positive** social **and** economic impacts created by the construction of a major dam and its associated reservoir.

5

[Turn over

MARKS

Question 8: Development and Health

Diagram Q8: Development indicators for selected developing countries

| Country | Indicators of Development | | | | | |
	GDP (US $ per capita)	Employment agriculture (%)	Adult literacy (%)	Birth rate (births per 1000)	Life expectancy at birth (in years)	Hospital beds (per 1000)
Mexico	15,400	14	93	18	76	1·7
Brazil	11,700	16	90	15	73	2·3
Cuba	10,200	20	99	10	78	5·1
Kenya	1,800	75	87	30	63	1·4
Malawi	800	90	75	40	53	1·3

(a)   Study Diagram Q8 above before answering this question.

In what ways does the information in the table suggest that the five countries are at different levels of development?

4

(b)   Suggest reasons for the wide variations in development which exist between developing countries. You may wish to refer to countries that you have studied.

6

MARKS

Question 9: Global Climate Change

Look at Diagram Q9.

Diagram Q9: Natural and Enhanced Greenhouse Effect

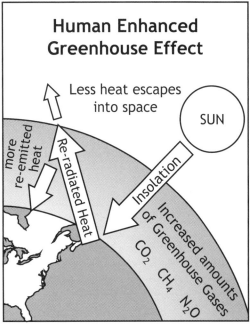

Many scientists believe that human activity has led to an enhanced greenhouse effect.

(a)   **Explain** the human factors that may lead to climate change.   4

(b)   **Discuss** a range of possible effects of climate change. You should support your answer with specific examples.   6

[Turn over

MARKS

Question 10: Trade, Aid and Geopolitics

Read the quotation in Diagram Q10a below.

Diagram Q10a: Quotation from Nelson Mandela (22nd November 2000)

"Where globalisation means, as it so often does, that the rich and powerful now have new means to further enrich and empower themselves at the cost of the poorer and weaker, we have a responsibility to protest in the name of universal freedom."

(a) **Explain** the social and economic impacts of unfair trade on people and countries in the **Developing World**.   4

Diagram Q10b: Fair Trade and Normal Coffee prices

(b) Study Diagram Q10b.

Using the information in Diagram Q10b, and also your knowledge of fair trade, **explain** how fair trade:

(i) helps to reduce inequalities in world trade; and

(ii) impacts on farming communities.   6

MARKS

Question 11: Energy

Diagram Q11: % Energy Production in Selected Countries

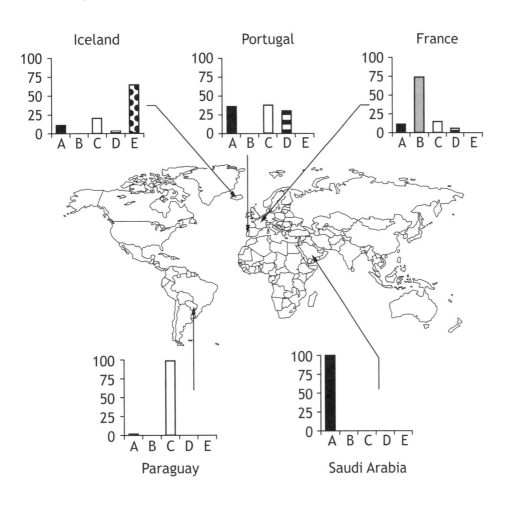

Key:

A ▪ Fossil Fuels (oil, gas and coal)

B ▪ Nuclear

C ☐ Hydroelectric Power (HEP)

D ▤ Other Renewables (solar and wind power)

E ▪ Geothermal Power

Study Diagram Q11.

(a)   Using the information in the diagram **suggest reasons** for the different patterns of energy production in the countries shown.　　4

(b)   Choose **one** renewable *and* **one** non-renewable approach to energy production, and for each approach, **evaluate** its effectiveness in meeting energy demands.　　6

SECTION 4 : APPLICATION OF GEOGRAPHICAL SKILLS – 10 marks   MARKS

Attempt the question

Question 12

> There is a proposal to develop the site at 468057 on the OS Map extract as an Outdoor and Environmental Education centre at Dalmellington, East Ayrshire.
>
> The specifications required for this development are listed below.
>
> Specifications for an Outdoor & Environmental Education Centre:
>
> - offer a range of land-based activities — hillwalking, orienteering, mountain biking and abseiling/rock-climbing
>
> - provide facilities for fishing and water-sports
>
> - allow opportunities for environmental education, fieldwork and conservation in the local area, eg biology and geography studies.

Study Diagram Q12a – Location of Proposed Development; OS Map (Extract 2144/EXP327: Dalmellington), Diagram Q12b, Diagram Q12c, Diagram Q12d and Diagram Q12e before answering this question.

Referring to map evidence from the OS Map extract, and other information from the sources, **discuss**:

(a)   the advantages **and** disadvantages of the proposed location; **and**

(b)   any possible impacts on the local area and East Ayrshire.   **10**

Diagram Q12a : Location of Proposed Development

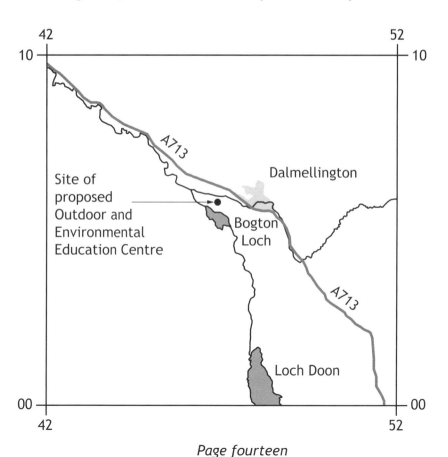

Question 12 (continued)   MARKS

Diagram Q12b : Photograph of Bogton Loch & Dalmellington Moss looking SW from GR 466065

Dalmellington Moss is a Scottish Wildlife Trust Nature Reserve. Rare heathers and moss along with birds such as curlew and snipe can be found here.

Auchenroy Hill

Bogton Loch is a Site of Special Scientific Interest because of the flora and fauna, including water birds, such as Teal and Reed Warblers, the Whooper swan and Greylag goose.

Diagram Q12c: Unemployment rates (%) for East Ayrshire and Scotland, 2008 – 2010

	2008	2009	2010
East Ayrshire	5·6	8·0	9·7
Scotland	4·5	5·9	7·6

Diagram Q12d: Population Change for Dalmellington and Burnton 2001 – 2010

Diagram Q12e: Where tourists spend their money in Ayrshire and Arran

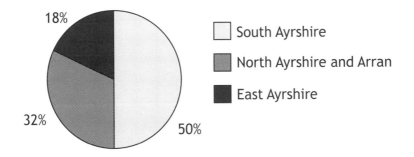

South Ayrshire

North Ayrshire and Arran

East Ayrshire

[END OF QUESTION PAPER]

Page fifteen

[BLANK PAGE]

DO NOT WRITE ON THIS PAGE

National
Qualifications
2015

X733/76/21

Geography
Ordnance Survey Map

THURSDAY, 21 MAY

9:00 AM – 11:15 AM

ORDNANCE SURVEY MAP

For Question 12

Note: The colours used in the printing of this map extract are indicated in the four little boxes at the top of the map extract. Each box should contain a colour; if any does not, the map is incomplete and should be returned to the Invigilator.

Ordnance Survey®

ROADS AND PATHS   Not necessarily rights of way

A 35	Motorway Service Area Junction Number
A 30	Dual carriageway
B 3074	Main road
	Secondary road
	Narrow road with passing places
	Road under construction
	Road generally more than 4 m wide
	Road generally less than 4 m wide
	Other road, drive or track, fenced and unfenced
	Gradient: steeper than 20% (1 in 5) 14% (1 in 7) to 20% (1 in 5)
Ferry	(V) Vehicle; (P) Passenger
	Path

RAILWAYS

	Multiple track Single track } Standard gauge
	Narrow gauge or Light Rapid Transit System (LRTS) and station
	Road over; road under; level crossing
	Cutting; tunnel; embankment
	Station, open to passengers; siding

PUBLIC RIGHTS OF WAY   Not shown on maps of Scotland

- - - - - - -	Footpath
	Bridleway
+ + + + +	Byway open to all traffic
	Restricted byway

The representation on this map of any other road, track or path
is no evidence of the existence of a right of way

OTHER PUBLIC ACCESS

• • •	Other routes with public access
	National Trail / Long Distance Route; Recreational route
- - - - - -	Permitted footpath } See note below
	Permitted bridleway

Footpaths and bridleways along which landowners
have permitted public use but which are not rights
of way. The agreement may be withdrawn.

• • •	Traffic-free cycle route
1	National cycle network route number – traffic free
1	National cycle network route number – on road

BOUNDARIES

— + — + —	National
— ·· — ·· —	County (England)
— — — —	Unitary Authority (UA), Metropolitan District (Met Dist), London Borough (LB) or District (Scotland & Wales are solely Unitary Authorities)
· · · · · ·	Civil Parish (CP) (England) or Community (C) (Wales)
	National Park

HISTORICAL FEATURES

✚	Site of antiquity
✗ 1066	Site of battle (with date)
VILLA	Roman
Castle	Non-Roman
	Visible earthwork

Magnetic North   Grid North   True North

Diagrammatic
only

GENERAL FEATURES

	Gravel pit		Sand pit
	Other pit or quarry		Landfill site or slag heap
	Slopes		
+	Place of worship		
	Current or former place of worship – with tower – with spire, minaret or dome		
□ ■	Building; important building		
■	Glasshouse		
▲	Youth hostel		
■	Bunkhouse / camping barn / other hostel		
	Bus or coach station		
⊥ ⊥	Lighthouse; disused lighthouse;		
⋏	Beacon		

⊥	Triangulation pillar
Ⅰ	Mast
⚡	Windmill; with or without sails
Ⅹ Ⅹ	Wind pump; wind turbine
pylon ·—· pole	Electricity transmission line
BP	Boundary post
BS	Boundary stone
CH	Clubhouse
FB	Footbridge
MP; MS	Milepost; milestone
Mon	Monument
PO	Post office
Pol Sta	Police station
Sch	School
TH	Town Hall
NTL	Normal tidal limit
- W; Spr	Well; spring

HEIGHTS AND NATURAL FEATURES

52 ·	Ground survey height
284	Air survey height

Surface heights are to the nearest metre above mean sea
level. Where two heights are shown, the first height is to the
base of the triangulation pillar and the second (in brackets) to
the highest natural point of the hill

Vertical face/cliff

Boulders	Loose rock	Outcrop	Scree

Water; mud

Sand; sand and shingle

VEGETATION

Vegetation limits are defined by positioning of symbols

♠ ♠	Coniferous trees
○ ○	Non-coniferous trees
	Coppice
	Orchard
	Scrub
	Bracken, heath or rough grassland
	Marsh, reeds or saltings

ACCESS LAND (England & Wales)

	Access land boundary and tint
	Access land in wooded area
ⓘ	Access information point
MANAGED ACCESS	Access permitted within managed controls, for example, local byelaws

Portrayal of access land on this map is intended as
a guide to land which is normally available for
access on foot, for example access land created
under the Countryside and Rights of Way Act 2000,
and land managed by the National Trust, Forestry
Commission and Woodland Trust.

Access for other activities may also exist. Some
restrictions will apply; some land will be excluded
from open access rights.

The depiction of rights of access does not imply or
express any warranty as to its accuracy or
completeness. Observe local signs and follow the
Countryside Code.

ACCESS LAND (Scotland)

	Land open to the public by permission of the owners. The agreement may be withdrawn.
	National Trust for Scotland Property; always open
	National Trust for Scotland Property; limited access – observe local signs
	Forestry Commission Land
	Woodland Trust Land

In Scotland, everyone has access rights in law over
most land and inland water, provided access is
exercised responsibly (Land Reform [Scotland] Act
2003). **This includes walking, cycling, horse-
riding and water access, for recreational and
educational purposes, and for crossing land or
water.** Access rights do not apply to motorised
activities, hunting, shooting or fishing, nor if your
dog is not under proper control.

OTHER ACCESS

DANGER AREA	Firing and test ranges in the area. Danger! Observe warning notices

TOURIST AND LEISURE INFORMATION

	Building of historic interest		Garden / arboretum		Preserved railway
	Cadw (Welsh heritage)		Golf course or links	PC	Public Convenience
	Camp site		Information centre		Public house/s
	Caravan site		Information centre, seasonal		Recreation / leisure / sports centre
	Camping and caravan site		Horse riding		Slipway
	Castle / fort		Museum		Telephone (public / motoring organisation / emergency)
	Cathedral / Abbey		Nature reserve		Theme / pleasure park
	Country park		National Trust property		Viewpoint
	Cycle trail		Other tourist feature		Visitor centre
	English Heritage property	P	Parking		Walks / trails
	Fishing	P&R	Park and ride, all year / seasonal		Water activites
	Forestry Commission visitor centre		Picnic site		World Heritage site or area

Scale 1:25 000

		0 Kilometres		1

1   ¾   ½   ¼   0 Miles   1

1 kilometre = 0·6214 mile   4 centimetres to 1 kilometre (one grid square)   1 Mile = 1·6093 kilometres

HIGHER

2016

H National Qualifications 2016

X733/76/11

Geography

FRIDAY, 6 MAY

9:00 AM – 11:15 AM

Total marks — 60

SECTION 1 — PHYSICAL ENVIRONMENTS — 15 marks

Attempt ALL questions.

SECTION 2 — HUMAN ENVIRONMENTS — 15 marks

Attempt ALL questions.

SECTION 3 — GLOBAL ISSUES — 20 marks

Attempt TWO questions.

SECTION 4 — APPLICATION OF GEOGRAPHICAL SKILLS — 10 marks

Attempt the question.

Credit will be given for appropriately labelled sketch maps and diagrams.

Write your answers clearly in the answer booklet provided. In the answer booklet you must clearly identify the question number you are attempting.

Use **blue** or **black** ink.

Before leaving the examination room you must give your answer booklet to the Invigilator; if you do not you may lose all the marks for this paper.

MARKS

SECTION 1 — PHYSICAL ENVIRONMENTS — 15 marks

Attempt ALL questions

Question 1

Study Maps Q1A and Q1B before answering this question.

(a)   **Compare** the rainfall patterns across West Africa; **and**

(b)   **suggest reasons** for the variations.   5

Map Q1A: Location of selected air masses and the ITCZ in January and July

Key:

mT   =   Maritime Tropical   cT   =   Continental Tropical

ITCZ   =   Inter Tropical Convergence Zone

MARKS

Question 1 (continued)

Map Q1B: Rainfall patterns in West Africa

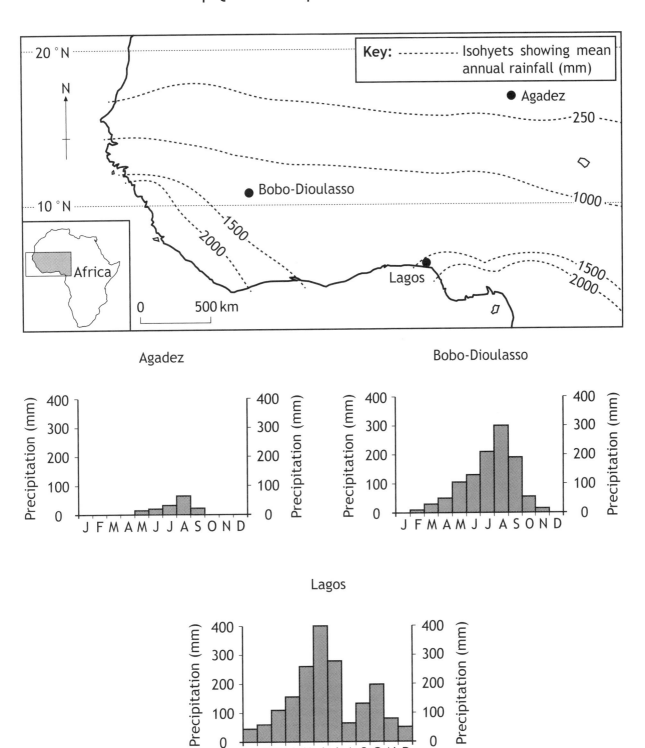

MARKS

Question 2

Read Diagram Q2.

Diagram Q2: Extract from Lake District Management Plan

> *The Lake District's varied scenery and historic environment provide for a wide range of sport, recreational and leisure activities . . . this has grown and changed over time.*
>
> *As the National Park continues to change, we need to monitor how access and recreation is being managed to ensure that a balance exists between the needs of everyone.*
>
> State of the Park Report 2005: Access and Recreation

Referring to a glaciated upland area you have studied:

(a) **explain** the environmental conflicts caused by the various land uses   ;   5

(b)   (i) **explain** the strategies used to manage these conflicts; and

      (ii) **comment on** the effectiveness of these strategies.   5

MARKS

SECTION 2 — HUMAN ENVIRONMENTS — 15 marks
Attempt ALL questions

Question 3

Look at Map Q3 before answering this question.

The Great Green Wall Initiative aims to reduce the impact of land degradation in the Sahel zone of Northern Africa.

(a) **Explain** techniques employed to manage rural land degradation in a rainforest **or** semi arid area that you have studied; **and**

(b) **comment on** the effectiveness of these techniques.   6

Map Q3: The Great Green Wall Initiative

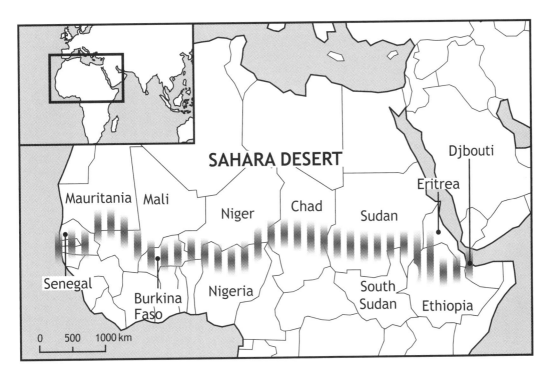

■ ■ ■ "Great Green Wall" of trees

Total distance: 7,775 km

Total area: 11,662,500 hectares

[Turn over

MARKS

Question 4

In November 2013, the Chairperson of Nigeria's National Population Commission resigned after questioning the accuracy of the data gathered about the country's population.

(a) **Discuss** how countries gather accurate population data.

3

(b) **Explain** why it is difficult to gather accurate population data in developing world countries.

6

SECTION 3 — GLOBAL ISSUES — 20 marks
Attempt TWO questions

[Turn over

MARKS

Question 5: River Basin Management

Map Q5A: Bangladesh

Map Q5B: Karnafuli River Basin

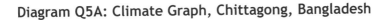

MARKS

Question 5: (continued)

Diagram Q5A: Climate Graph, Chittagong, Bangladesh

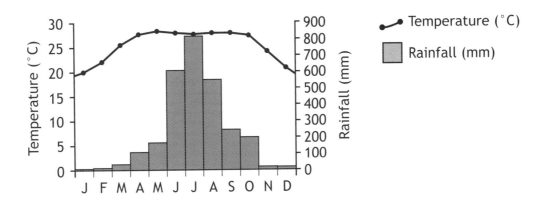

Diagram Q5B: Population growth in Bangladesh

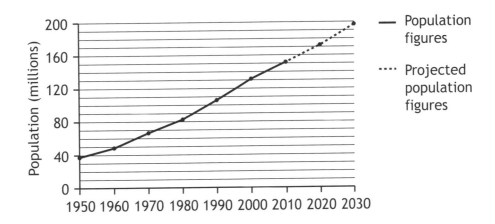

Diagram Q5C: Selected statistics, Bangladesh

Access to Improved drinking water	84%
Access to Improved sanitation	55%
Access to Electricity	62%
Main Industries	Textiles; Agriculture (rice/jute); Construction

(a) Study Map Q5A, Map Q5B, Diagram Q5A, Diagram Q5B, and Diagram Q5C.

Explain why there is a need for water management in the Karnafuli River Basin.

6

(b) Referring to a water control project you have studied, **discuss** the positive **and** negative **environmental** impacts created by the construction of a major dam and its associated reservoir.

4

MARKS

Question 6: Development and Health

Look at Table Q6.

Table Q6: Selected Developing Countries

Country	GNI (Gross National Income) per capita (US$)
Venezuela	13,600
Nigeria	2,800
Malawi	900

(a) **Explain** why using only **one** development indicator, such as Gross National Income (GNI) per capita, may fail to reflect accurately the true quality of life within a country.   3

(b) Referring to specific Primary Health Care strategies you have studied:

   (i) **explain** how these strategies meet the health care needs of the people in a developing country; **and**

   (ii) **comment on** the effectiveness of these strategies.   7

MARKS

Question 7: Global Climate Change

(a) **Explain** the **physical** causes of climate change.

4

(b) Study Diagram Q7.

Explain possible strategies for managing climate change.

6

Diagram Q7: Levels of managing Climate Change

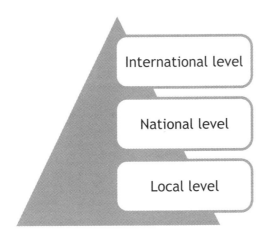

International level

National level

Local level

[Turn over

Question 8: Trade, Aid and Geopolitics

Table Q8: Trade Patterns of Selected Countries

Country	Population (millions)	GDP per Capita (US$)	Exports (billions US$)	Imports (billions US$)	Balance of Trade (billions US$)
Australia	23	67,304	252	245	+7
USA	318	51,704	1,575	2,273	−698
Germany	81	41,866	1,493	1,233	+260
UK	64	39,161	475	646	−171
Saudi Arabia	30	24,524	376	147	+229
Botswana	2	16,400	3	7	−4
Russia	144	14,302	515	341	+174
Brazil	201	11,358	245	241	+4
South Africa	53	7,525	91	99	−8
China	1,361	6,071	2,210	1,772	+438
Ghana	25	3,500	13	18	−5
India	1,241	1,499	318	516	−198
Zimbabwe	13	600	7	4	+3

(Data from CIA World Fact book — 2013)

(a) Study Table Q8 above.

To what extent does the data in the table show inequalities in the pattern of world trade?

4

(b) Give reasons for the inequalities in the pattern of trade shown in the table or between other countries that you have studied.

6

Question 9: Energy

MARKS

Graph Q9A: Total UK energy consumption (1970-2030)

(a)　Look at Graph Q9A above.

Suggest reasons for the changes in energy consumption in the UK.　　5

Diagram Q9B: Hydraulic Fracturing ("Fracking") to extract shale gas

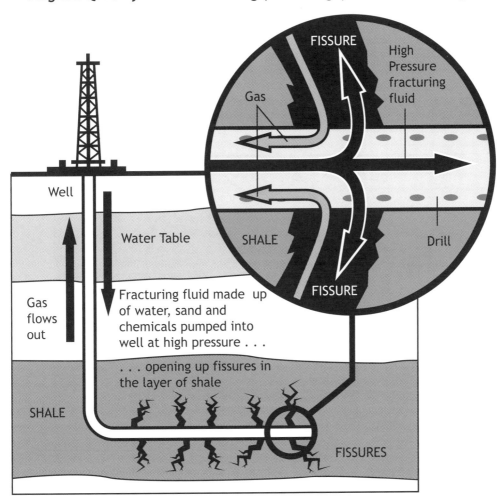

(b)　Look carefully at Diagram Q9B above.

Discuss the advantages **and** disadvantages of hydraulic fracturing ("fracking"), or any other **non**-renewable source of energy you have studied, in meeting the energy demands of a country.　　5

MARKS

SECTION 4 – APPLICATION OF GEOGRAPHICAL SKILLS – 10 marks

Attempt the question

Question 10

East Sussex County Council is building a new by-pass from 743091 to 776111 (The Bexhill–Hastings Link Road), however, not everyone is pleased with this decision.

Study the OS Map (Extract No 2214/EXP124: Hastings and Bexhill), Map Q10, Diagram Q10A, Diagram Q10B, Diagram Q10C and Diagram Q10D, before answering this question.

Referring to evidence from the OS map extract, and other information from the sources, **discuss**:

(a)   the advantages **and** disadvantages of the proposed route; **and**

(b)   any possible impacts on the surrounding area.

10

Diagram Q10A: Part of Sussex Wildlife Trust's response to the new road proposal

"Sussex Wildlife Trust strongly objects to the Bexhill–Hastings Link Road Scheme. The proposals do not represent sustainable development. The scheme will result in unacceptable environmental damage."

Map Q10: Route of the Bexhill to Hastings Link Road

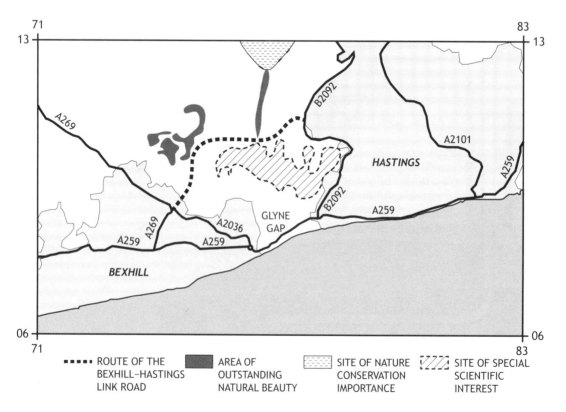

Question 10 (continued)

MARKS

Diagram Q10B: Average Hourly Traffic Flow on the A259 at Glyne Gap 768082 June 2012

Diagram Q10C: Number of days that safe air pollution levels were exceeded at Glyne Gap 768082 June 2011 to June 2013

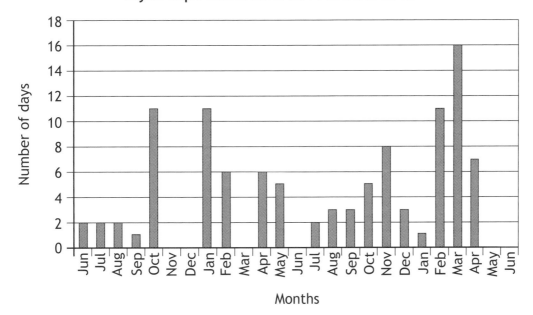

Diagram Q10D: Predicted visual impact on the Combe Havan Valley (View East from 757107) towards Adam's farm

Current View

Artist impression of view in 2020

[END OF QUESTION PAPER]

[BLANK PAGE]

DO NOT WRITE ON THIS PAGE

National
Qualifications
2016

X733/76/21

Geography
Ordnance Survey Map

FRIDAY, 6 MAY

9:00 AM – 11:15 AM

ORDNANCE SURVEY MAP

For Question 10

Note: The colours used in the printing of this map extract are indicated in the four little boxes at the top of the map extract. Each box should contain a colour; if any does not, the map is incomplete and should be returned to the Invigilator.

Ordnance Survey

1:25 000 Scale
Explorer Series

ROADS AND PATHS   Not necessarily rights of way

Motorway ◇ Service Area ▣ Junction Number	
A 35	Dual carriageway
A 30	Main road
B 3074	Secondary road
	Narrow road with passing places
	Road under construction
	Road generally more than 4 m wide
	Road generally less than 4 m wide
	Other road, drive or track, fenced and unfenced
→→→	Gradient: steeper than 20% (1 in 5) 14% (1 in 7) to 20% (1 in 5)
Ferry	Ferry; Ferry P – passenger only
	Path

RAILWAYS

Multiple track / Single track	Standard gauge
○	Narrow gauge or Light Rapid Transit System (LRTS) and station
	Road over; road under; level crossing
	Cutting; tunnel; embankment
	Station, open to passengers; siding

PUBLIC RIGHTS OF WAY   Not shown on maps of Scotland

- - - - - -	Footpath
— — —	Bridleway
+−+−+−+	Byway open to all traffic
−·−·−·	Restricted byway-not for use by mechanically propelled vehicles

The representation on this map of any other road, track or path is no evidence of the existence of a right of way

OTHER PUBLIC ACCESS

● ● ●	Other routes with public access

The exact nature of the rights on these routes and the existence of any restrictions may be checked with the local highway authority. Alignments are based on the best information available

◆ ◆ ◆	Recreational route
◆ ◆ ◆ 🚶	National Trail / (🚴) Long Distance Route
- - - - - -	Permissive footpath } See note below
— — —	Permissive bridleway }

Footpaths and bridleways along which landowners have permitted public use but which are not rights of way. The agreement may be withdrawn.

● ● ●	Traffic-free cycle route
1 ■	National cycle network route number – traffic free; on road

BOUNDARIES

—+—+—	National
— — —	County (England)
— — —	Unitary Authority (UA), Metropolitan District (Met Dist), London Borough (LB) or District (Scotland & Wales are solely Unitary Authorities)
··········	Civil Parish (CP) (England) or Community (C) (Wales)
— —	National Park

HISTORICAL FEATURES

✛	Site of antiquity
⚔ 1066	Site of battle (with date)
VILLA	Roman
Castle	Non-Roman
◦ ⊞	Visible earthwork

Information provided by English Heritage for England and the Royal Commissions on the Ancient and Historical Monuments for Scotland and Wales

GENERAL FEATURES

◉ Gravel pit	⌒ Sand pit
◉ Other pit or quarry	◉ Landfill site or slag/spoil heap
▥▥▥ Slopes	
+ Place of worship	
▲ Current or former place of worship – with tower	
■ – with spire, minaret or dome	
▭ ▭ Building; important building	
■ Glasshouse	
▲ Youth hostel	
■ Bunkhouse / camping barn / other hostel	
▭ Bus or coach station	
✦ ✦ Lighthouse; disused lighthouse;	
⊻ Beacon	

Ĭ		Triangulation pillar
Ŧ		Mast
✗		Windmill; with or without sails
⅄ ⅄		Wind pump; wind turbine
pylon ⸱ pole		Electricity transmission line
BP		Boundary post
BS		Boundary stone
CG		Cattle grid
CH		Clubhouse
FB		Footbridge
MP; MS		Milepost; milestone
Mon		Monument
PO		Post office
Pol Sta		Police station
Sch		School
TH		Town hall
NTL		Normal tidal limit
W; Spr		Well; spring

HEIGHTS AND NATURAL FEATURES

52 ·	Ground survey height
284	Air survey height

Surface heights are to the nearest metre above mean sea level. Where two heights are shown, the first height is to the base of the triangulation pillar and the second (in brackets) to the highest natural point of the hill

Vertical face/cliff

Boulders   Loose rock   Outcrop   Scree

	Water; mud
	Sand; sand and shingle

VEGETATION

Vegetation limits are defined by positioning of symbols

	Coniferous trees
	Non-coniferous trees
	Coppice
	Orchard
	Scrub
	Bracken, heath or rough grassland
	Marsh, reeds or saltings

ACCESS LAND

DANGER AREA	Firing and test ranges in the area. Danger! Observe warning notices
MANAGED ACCESS	Access permitted within managed controls, for example, local byelaws.

England and Wales

	Access land boundary and tint
	Access land in wooded area
🛈	Access information point

Portrayal of access land on this map is intended as a guide to land which is normally available for access on foot, for example access land created under the Countryside and Rights of Way Act 2000, and land managed by the National Trust, Forestry Commission and Woodland Trust.

Access for other activities may also exist. Some restrictions will apply; some land will be excluded from open access rights.

The depiction of rights of access does not imply or express any warranty as to its accuracy or completeness. Observe local signs and follow the Countryside Code.

Scotland

◪	National Trust for Scotland, always open
◪	National Trust for Scotland, limited access – observe local signs
◪	Forestry Commission Land
◪	Woodland Trust Land

In Scotland, everyone has access rights in law over most land and inland water, provided access is exercised responsibly (Land Reform [Scotland] Act 2003). **This includes walking, cycling, horse- riding and water access, for recreational and educational purposes, and for crossing land or water.** Access rights do not apply to motorised activities, hunting, shooting or fishing, nor if your dog is not under proper control.

TOURIST AND LEISURE INFORMATION

Building of historic interest	Forestry Commission visitor centre	Preserved railway
Boat trips	Garden / arboretum	PC Public Convenience
Boat hire	Golf course or links	Public house/s
Cadw (Welsh heritage)	Historic Scotland	Recreation / leisure / sports centre
Camp site/Caravan site	Information centre, seasonal	Slipway
Castle / fort	Horse riding	Telephone (public/ roadside assistance/ emergency)
Cathedral / Abbey	Museum	Theme / pleasure park
Craft Centre	Mountain bike trail	Viewpoint
Country park	Nature reserve	Visitor centre
Cycle hire	National Trust property	Walks / trails
Cycle trail	Other tourist feature	Water activites
English Heritage property	Parking / Park and ride, all year / seasonal	World Heritage site or area
Fishing	Picnic site	

Scale 1: 25 000

1 kilometre = 0·6214 mile   4 centimetres to 1 kilometre (one grid square)   1 Mile = 1·6093 kilometres

HIGHER

2017

National Qualifications 2017

X733/76/11

Geography

FRIDAY, 26 MAY

9:00 AM – 11:15 AM

Total marks — 60

SECTION 1 — PHYSICAL ENVIRONMENTS — 15 marks

Attempt ALL questions.

SECTION 2 — HUMAN ENVIRONMENTS — 15 marks

Attempt ALL questions.

SECTION 3 — GLOBAL ISSUES — 20 marks

Attempt TWO questions.

SECTION 4 — APPLICATION OF GEOGRAPHICAL SKILLS — 10 marks

Attempt the question.

Credit will be given for appropriately labelled sketch maps and diagrams.

Write your answers clearly in the answer booklet provided. In the answer booklet you must clearly identify the question number you are attempting.

Use **blue** or **black** ink.

Before leaving the examination room you must give your answer booklet to the Invigilator; if you do not you may lose all the marks for this paper.

MARKS

SECTION 1 — PHYSICAL ENVIRONMENTS — 15 marks
Attempt ALL questions

Question 1

Diagram Q1: Glaciated Landscape

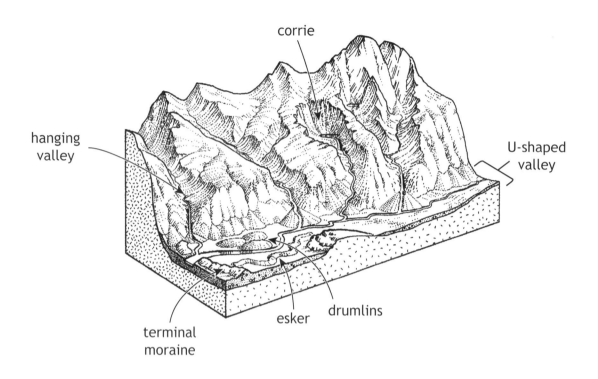

corrie

hanging valley

U-shaped valley

esker   drumlins

terminal moraine

Study Diagram Q1.

Explain the formation of **one** erosional landform **and one** depositional landform from Diagram Q1.

You may wish to use an annotated diagram or diagrams.

7

Question 2

Explain why there is a surplus of solar energy in the tropical latitudes and a deficit of solar energy towards the poles.

You may wish to use an annotated diagram or diagrams.

4

MARKS

Question 3

Diagram Q3: A typical gley soil profile

A - Top soil

B - Sub soil

C - Parent material

Look at Diagram Q3.

Explain the main conditions and processes which have led to the formation of a **gley** soil.   4

[Turn over

MARKS

SECTION 2 — HUMAN ENVIRONMENTS — 15 marks
Attempt ALL questions

Question 4

With reference to a migration flow you have studied:

(a)   **explain** the push **and** pull factors for this migration; **and**   4

(b)   **discuss** the impacts of this migration on **either** the donor **or** the receiving country.   3

Question 5

Referring to **either** a named rainforest **or** a semi-arid area you have studied, **discuss** the impacts of land degradation on the area.   4

Question 6

Evaluate the effectiveness of the strategies used to manage traffic in a developed world city you have studied.   4

SECTION 3 — GLOBAL ISSUES — 20 marks
Attempt TWO questions

[Turn over

MARKS

Question 7: River Basin Management

(a) **Explain** the physical factors that need to be considered when selecting a site for a dam and its associated reservoir.

4

(b) **Discuss** the adverse socio-economic **and** environmental consequences of a named river management project that you have studied.

6

MARKS

Question 8: Development and Health

"Of the 106 countries with ongoing malaria transmission in 2000, 57 achieved reductions in new malaria cases of at least 75% by 2015. Eighteen countries reduced their malaria cases by 50—75%."

World Health Organisation - World Malaria Report 2015.

For a water-related disease you have studied:

(a)   **explain** the strategies used to manage the disease; **and**

(b)   **comment** on the effectiveness of these strategies.   **10**

[Turn over

MARKS

Question 9: Global Climate Change

> "The impacts of global warming are likely to be 'severe and irreversible', a major report by the UN has warned."
>
> BBC News

(a) **Discuss** a range of possible impacts of climate change. You should support your answer with specific examples. **6**

(b) Many strategies have been implemented to both reduce greenhouse gas emissions and to manage the effects of climate change.

With reference to strategies you have studied, **comment on** their effectiveness. **4**

MARKS

Question 10: Trade, Aid and Geopolitics

Look at Table Q10.

Table Q10: World Trade Statistics 2014

Area	Share of exports (%)	Value of Exports ($ million)
Developed Countries	57	10,362,324
Developing Countries	40	7,272,568
Least Developed Countries	3	291,763

(a)   **Discuss** the social and economic impacts of trade inequalities on the world's poorest countries.   4

(b)   **Explain** the advantages and disadvantages of trading alliances. You should support your answer with specific examples.   6

[Turn over

MARKS

Question 11: Energy

Look at Diagram Q11a.

Diagram Q11a: World energy consumption 1971–2013

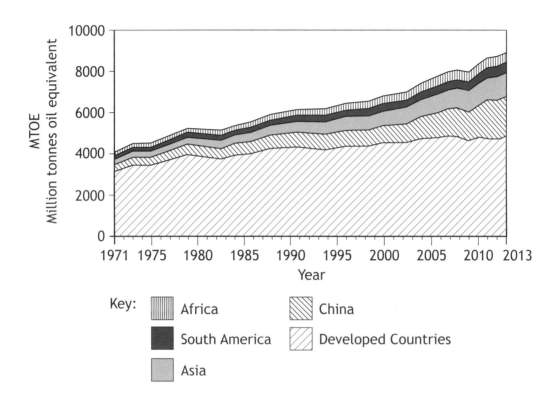

(a) **Suggest reasons** for the increasing energy demand in Developing Countries.   5

Look at Diagram Q11b.

Diagram Q11b: Norway: Source of Electrical Generation 2012

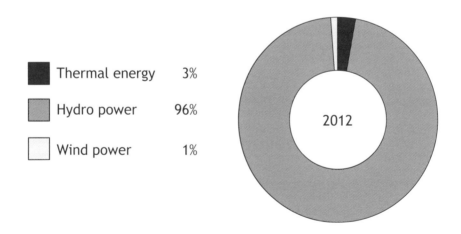

(b) **Discuss** the effectiveness of Hydro Electric Power (HEP), or any other renewable source of energy you have studied, in meeting energy demands. You may wish to refer to one or more countries in your answer.   5

[Turn over for next question

DO NOT WRITE ON THIS PAGE

SECTION 4 — APPLICATION OF GEOGRAPHICAL SKILLS — 10 marks

MARK

Attempt the question

Question 12

Planning permission has been granted to create 300 new homes to the south of Highbridge, which is a small town in the district of Sedgemoor. The development will include a new primary school for 210 pupils, outdoor play facilities and public spaces. The site will also provide opportunities for new walkways and a cycle route into Highbridge.

Study the OS Map (Extract No 2249/182) Diagram Q12A, Diagram Q12B, Diagram Q12C and Diagram Q12D before answering this question.

Referring to evidence from the OS Map extract and information from the other sources:

(a) **discuss** the suitability of the site, shown on Diagram Q12A for the proposed housing development; **and**

(b) **suggest** any social, economic or environmental impacts this development may have on the local area.

10

Diagram Q12A: Proposed site for New Housing Development in Highbridge, Sedgemoor District

Question 12 (continued)

Diagram Q12B: Location of Highbridge

Diagram Q12C: Population of Sedgemoor District

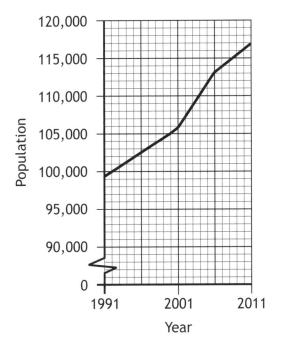

Diagram Q12D: News Article from Yeovil Express, October 2015

YEOVIL EXPRESS

Hinkley Point C is good news for local area

The expansion of the Nuclear Power Station will provide 25,000 new jobs to the area during construction. EDF Energy has also been busy putting into place the infrastructure that will help deliver the project and reduce its impact for the local community. £16 million has been invested in improving the local road network in Bridgwater and surrounding areas

[END OF QUESTION PAPER]

[BLANK PAGE]

DO NOT WRITE ON THIS PAGE

National
Qualifications
2017

X733/76/21

Geography
Ordnance Survey Map

FRIDAY, 26 MAY

9:00 AM – 11:15 AM

ORDNANCE SURVEY MAP

For Question 12

Note: The colours used in the printing of this map extract are indicated in the four little boxes at the top of the map extract. Each box should contain a colour; if any does not, the map is incomplete and should be returned to the Invigilator.

Ordnance Survey

1:50 000 Scale
Landranger Series

ROADS AND PATHS

Not necessarily rights of way

Junction number
Service area — Elevated

Motorway (dual carriageway)

Unfenced
A 470

Primary Route
(A network of recommended through routes which complement the motorway system)

Dual carriageway
A 493

Main road

Footbridge

Road under construction

B 4518

Secondary road

A 855 Bridge B 885

Narrow road with passing places

Road generally more than 4m wide

Road generally less than 4m wide

Path / Other road, drive or track

Gradient: steeper than 20% (1 in 5),
14% to 20% (1 in 7 to 1 in 5)

Gates, Road tunnel

Ferry P Ferry V

Ferry (passenger), Ferry (vehicle)

RAILWAYS

Track multiple or single

Bridges, footbridge

Track under construction

LC Level crossing

Siding

Viaduct, embankment

Tunnel, cuttings

a Station, (a) principal

Narrow gauge, tramway
or light rail system

Light rail station

WATER FEATURES

Marsh or salting

Cliff

Slopes

Towpath Lock

Shingle

Aqueduct Canal Ford Beacon Flat rock Lighthouse (in use)

Sand Lighthouse (disused)

Weir Normal tidal limit Dunes

Lake Footbridge Bridge Mud Low water mark

High water mark

Canal (dry)

HEIGHTS

1 metre = 3·2808 feet

50 Contours are at 10 metres vertical interval

144 Heights are to the nearest metre above mean sea level

Where two heights are shown, the first is the height of the natural ground in the location of the triangulation pillar, and the second (in brackets) to a separate point which is the natural summit.

ROCK FEATURES

Outcrop

Cliff

Scree

PUBLIC RIGHTS OF WAY

Footpath

Bridleway

Restricted byway (not for use by mechanically propelled vehicles)

Byway open to all traffic

The symbols show the defined route so far as the scale of mapping will allow.

The representation on this map of any other road, track or path is no evidence of the existence of a right of way. Not shown on maps of Scotland

Danger Area Firing and Test Ranges in the area. Danger! Observe warning notices.

OTHER PUBLIC ACCESS

Other route with public access (not normally shown in urban areas). Alignments are based on the best information available. These routes are not shown on maps of Scotland.

On-road cycle route

Traffic-free cycle route

4 National Cycle Network number

8 Regional Cycle Network number

National Trail, Scotland's Great Trails, European Long Distance Path and selected Recreational Routes

BOUNDARIES

National

District

County, Unitary Authority, Metropolitan District or London Borough

National Park

ANTIQUITIES

+ Site of antiquity

Site of Battle (with date)

Visible earthwork

VILLA Roman

Castle Non-Roman

TOURIST INFORMATION

Camp site / caravan site

Garden/aboretum

Golf course or links

i Information centre (all year / seasonal)

Nature reserve

P P&R Parking, Park and ride (all year / seasonal)

Picnic site

Recreation / leisure / sports centre

Selected places of tourist interest

Phone, public / emergency

Viewpoint

Visitor centre

Walks / Trails

World Heritage site or area

Youth hostel

LAND FEATURES

Electricity transmission line (pylons shown at standard spacing)

Pipe line (arrow indicates direction of flow)

ru ruin Buildings

Important building (selected)

Bus or coach station

Current or former place of worship with tower / with spire, minaret or dome

+ Place of worship

Glass structure

H Heliport

Triangulation pillar

Mast

Wind pump

Wind turbine

Windmill with or without sails

Graticule intersection at 5' intervals

Cutting, embankment

Landfill site or slag/spoil heap

Coniferous wood

Non-coniferous wood

Mixed wood

Orchard

Park or ornamental ground

Forestry Commission land

National Trust (always open / limited access, observe local signs)

Natural Resources Wales

National Trust for Scotland (always open / limited access, observe local signs)

ABBREVIATIONS

Br	Bridge	MS	Milestone
Cemy	Cemetery	Mus	Museum
CG	Cattle grid	P	Post office
CH	Clubhouse	PC	Public convenience (in rural areas)
Fm	Farm	PH	Public house
Hospl	Hospital	Sch	School
Ho	House	TH	Town Hall, Guildhall or equivalent
MP	Milepost	Univ	University

Scale 1: 50 000
2 centimetres to 1 kilometre (one grid square)

2 1 0 Kilometres 1 2 3

1 0 Miles 1 2

1 kilometre = 0·6214 mile

1 mile = 1·6093 kilometres

Grid North Magnetic North True North

Diagrammatic only

Extract No 2249/182

Four colours should appear above; if not then please return to the invigilator.

HIGHER

Answers

SQA HIGHER GEOGRAPHY 2017

General Marking Principles for Higher Geography

This information is provided to help you understand the general principles you must apply when marking candidate responses to questions in this Paper. These principles must be read in conjunction with the detailed marking instructions, which identify the key features required in candidate responses.

a) Marks for each candidate response must always be assigned in line with these General Marking Principles and the Detailed Marking Instructions for this assessment.

b) Marking should always be positive. This means that, for each candidate response, marks are accumulated for the demonstration of relevant skills, knowledge and understanding: they are not deducted from a maximum on the basis of errors or omissions.

c) Where the candidate violates the rubric of the paper and answers two parts in one section, both responses should be marked and the better mark recorded.

d) Marking must be consistent. Never make a hasty judgement on a response based on length, quality of hand writing or a confused start.

e) Use the full range of marks available for each question.

f) The Detailed Marking Instructions are not an exhaustive list. Other relevant points should be credited.

g) For credit to be given, points must relate to the question asked. Where candidates give points of knowledge without specifying the context, these should be rewarded unless it is clear that they do not refer to the context of the question.

h) For knowledge/understanding marks to be awarded, points must be:
   a. relevant to the issue in the question
   b. developed (by providing additional detail, exemplification, reasons or evidence)
   c. used to respond to the demands of the question (ie evaluate, analyse, etc)

Marking principles for each question type

There are a range of types of question which could be asked within this question paper. For each, the following provides an overview of marking principles, and an example for each.

Explain

Questions which ask candidates to explain or suggest reasons for the cause or impact of something, or require them to refer to causal connections and relationships: candidates must do more than describe to gain credit here.

Where this occurs in a question asking about a landscape feature, candidates should refer to the processes leading to landscape formation.

Where candidates are provided with sources, they should make use of these and refer to them within their answer for full marks.

Where candidates provide a purely descriptive answer, or one where development is limited, no more than half marks should be awarded for the question.

Other questions look for higher-order skills to be demonstrated and will use command words such as analyse, evaluate, to what extent does, discuss.

Analyse

Analysis involves identifying parts, the relationship between them, and their relationships with the whole. It can also involve drawing out and relating implications.

An analysis mark should be awarded where a candidate uses their knowledge and understanding/a source, to identify relevant components (eg of an idea, theory, argument, etc) and clearly show at least one of the following:

- links between different components
- links between component(s) and the whole
- links between component(s) and related concepts
- similarities and contradictions
- consistency and inconsistency
- different views/interpretations
- possible consequences/implications
- the relative importance of components
- understanding of underlying order or structure

Where candidates are asked to analyse they should identify parts of a topic or issue and refer to the interrelationships between, or impacts of, various factors, eg analyse the soil-forming properties which lead to the formation of a gley soil. Candidates would be expected to refer to how the various soil formatting properties contributed to the formation.

Evaluate

Where candidates are asked to evaluate, they should be making a judgement of the success, failure, or impact of something based on criteria. Candidates would be expected to briefly describe the strategy/project being evaluated before offering an evidenced conclusion.

Account for

Where candidates are being asked to account for, they are required to give reasons, often (but not exclusively) from a resource, eg for a change in trade figures, a need for water management, or differences in development between contrasting developing countries.

Discuss

These questions are looking for candidates to explore ideas about a project, or the impact of a change. Candidates will be expected to consider different views on an issue/argument. This might not be a balanced argument, but there should be a range of impacts or ideas within the answer.

To what extent

This asks candidates to consider the impact of a management strategy or strategies they have explored. Candidates would be expected to briefly describe the strategy/project being evaluated before offering an evidenced conclusion. Candidates do not need to offer an overall opinion based on a variety of strategies, but should assess each separately.

General Marking Information for students

When answering a question, you should ensure that you read the question carefully before you start. You should look at the command word to ensure you answer the question correctly, eg if the question asks you to explain, then you must give reasons to support your response. Remember that there are no describe questions so, if your answers do not contain more than a descriptive point, it will be difficult to achieve any marks. If a question asks for two points of view to be covered, for example, advantages and disadvantages, then both must be covered for full marks. If the question is out of six and only the advantages are covered, then a maximum mark of four or five might be awarded. If a named area or example is asked for, then you may lose a mark(s) if you give a general response to the question. There are often more points covered (worth a mark each) in the following answers than will be required. For example, there could be six or seven points listed for a five-mark answer. Since the question is only worth five marks then any five of the six points could gain the five marks.

HIGHER GEOGRAPHY
2015

Section 1: Physical Environments

Question	General marking principle for this type of question	Max mark	Specific marking instruction for this question
1.	Award 1 mark for a developed explanation, two limited explanations, or for a description of the discharge with limited explanation. Award a maximum of 2 marks for description of the discharge with 1 mark being awarded for every two descriptive points being made. Markers should accept all relevant and appropriate explanations for the source provided.	4	Slight increase in discharge until 09.00 hours in response to rain which started to fall at 07.00 hours (**1 mark**). At first, this rain would have been intercepted by vegetation and have infiltrated the soil (**1 mark**). There is a steep rising limb up to a peak discharge of 100 cumecs at 18.00 hours (**1 mark**). This water would have filled up storages in the soil due to throughflow and groundwater (**1 mark**) — as the soil became saturated, surface run-off increased causing a peak (**1 mark**). The rising limb becomes less steep briefly between 13.00 and 15.00 hours, caused by a marked reduction in rain to 4mm around 10.00 hours (**1 mark**). There is a short lag time of 5 hours which could be due to deforestation/steep slopes/impermeable rock (**1 mark**). A high number of tributaries may lead to the short lag time as water is transported more rapidly by surface run-off (**1 mark**). The river discharge quickly decreases, shown by a steep falling/recession limb down to because of no more rainfall after 15.00 hours (**1 mark**).
2.	Award a maximum of 4 marks for either feature. Award a maximum of 6 marks if no diagrams are used. Check any diagram(s) for relevant points not present in the text and award accordingly. Well-annotated diagrams that explain conditions and processes can gain full marks. Award a maximum of 1 mark for three or more correctly named, but undeveloped, processes. Award a maximum of 2 marks for fully developed processes for any one feature. Answers which are purely descriptive, or have no mention of any processes or conditions, should achieve no more than 2 marks in total, with 1 mark being awarded for every two descriptive points being made. **1 mark** Limited explanation — the use of the names of at least two processes in context with no development of these. **2 marks** The use of the names of at least two processes with development of these, but no other reference to conditions. **OR** Limited use of the names of at least two processes, with at least two descriptive points about the landscape formation.	7	Headland with weaknesses such as joints, faults or cracks is eroded by the sea to form firstly caves (**1 mark**). Erosion takes place due to hydraulic action — pounding waves compress trapped air in the rocks, creating an explosive blast which weakens and loosens rock fragments (**1 mark**), abrasion/corrasion — rock fragments thrown against the headland create a sandblasting (abrasive) action, wearing away the rock (**1 mark**), solution/corrosion — carbonic acid in sea water weathering limestone and chalk (**1 mark**), attrition — rock fragments slowly being ground down by friction from wave action into smaller and rounder pieces (**1 mark**). In some cases, a blowhole can form in the roof of the cave as compressed air is pushed upwards by the power of the waves, causing vertical erosion (**1 mark**). Over time, erosion on both sides of the headland cuts through the backwall and enlarges the cave to create an arch (**1 mark**). Continued erosion at the foot of the headland and the effects of vibrations on the roof of the arch weakens it, eventually resulting in the collapse of the arch roof, leaving a stack isolated from the headland (**1 mark**). These low ridges of sand or shingle slowly extend from the shore across a bay or a river estuary and are caused by longshore drift (**1 mark**). This lateral movement occurs when waves, driven by the prevailing wind, pushes material up the beach; known as the swash (**1 mark**). The returning backwash is dragged back by gravity down the beach at right angles (**1 mark**). Material slowly builds up to appear above the water and begins to grow longer and wider. The spit develops as long as the supply of deposits is greater than the amount of erosion (**1 mark**). Spits form when there is a change in direction on a coastline, which allows a sheltered area for deposition (**1 mark**). They can also develop at a bay or a river estuary where the river current prevents the spit from extending right across the bay or estuary (**1 mark**). The shape can change through time to become curved or hooked at the end in response to changes in wind direction and currents (**1 mark**).

Question	General marking principle for this type of question	Max mark	Specific marking instruction for this question
2.	*(continued)* **3 marks** Two developed processes with limited explanation of how the feature forms over time. **4 marks** Two named processes with development of these, with two further statements explaining the formation of the feature.		
3.	Award 1 mark for each developed explanation or for two less developed points. Candidates should be awarded 1 mark if they only name and locate at least two cells/winds, not credited elsewhere. Credit any valid responses.	4	Warm air rises at the Equator and travels in the upper atmosphere to around 30° N and S, cools and sinks **(1 mark)**. Air moves from the tropical high to the low pressure area at the equator creating the Hadley Cell/Trade Winds **(1 mark)**. Cold air sinking at the poles moves to 60°N/S to form the Polar Cell/Polar Easterlies **(1 mark)**. The cold air from the poles meets warmer air from the tropics, causing air to rise creating the Ferrel Cell low pressure **(1 mark)**. Air is moved from the tropical HP, towards LP at the polar front, forming the westerlies **(1 mark)**. This convergence causes the air to rise, with some of this flowing in the upper atmosphere to the Poles where it sinks, forming the Polar Cell. Easterly winds blow away from the high pressure at the Pole **(1 mark)**. Warm air from the Equator is distributed to higher and cooler latitudes and cold air from the Poles distributed to lower and warmer latitudes **(1 mark)**. Due to the Coriolis effect winds are deflected to the right in the northern hemisphere **(1 mark)**. Credit should be awarded for answers which refer to the Rossby Waves and/or the Jet Stream.

Section 2: Human Environments

Question	General marking principle for this type of question	Max mark	Specific marking instruction for this question
4.	Candidates should discuss the positive or negative consequences of the predicted population structure in 2050. For 1 mark, candidates may give one detailed consequence, or a limited description/explanation of two factors. Detail may include relevant exemplification of a problem. A maximum of 2 marks should be awarded for answers consisting entirely of limited descriptive/explanatory points, with two such points required for 1 mark. Care should be taken not to ensure consequences are relevant to developing countries. Credit any other valid responses.	5	*Possible answers may include:* • The total population will increase significantly putting additional pressure on services and resources like education **(1 mark)**. Housing in Ghana, like many developing countries, is already overcrowded. This problem is likely to continue, with many people being forced to live in shanty town housing **(1 mark)**. • There will be a much larger potential workforce which may attract multinational companies to the country **(1 mark)**. An increase in the active age group, however, could also result in higher levels of unemployment or underemployment **(1 mark)**. • In total, there will be twice as many children, so significant investment in maternity hospitals, immunisation programmes and education will be needed **(1 mark)**. It will be necessary to build more schools and train more teachers to support the growing number of young people **(1 mark)**. • Government policies may promote smaller families or encourage emigration to reduce the problems of over-population **(1 mark)**. • With life expectancy increasing, it will also be necessary to invest in healthcare to meet the needs of an ageing population in the future **(1 mark)**.

Question	General marking principle for this type of question	Max mark	Specific marking instruction for this question
5.	Answers will depend on the case study referenced by the candidate. Marks may be awarded as follows: For 1 mark, candidates may give one detailed explanation, or a limited description/explanation of two factors. A maximum of 2 marks should be awarded for answers consisting entirely of limited descriptive points, with two such points required for 1 mark. A maximum of 4 marks should be awarded if the answer does not clearly relate to a specific case study. Credit any other valid responses.	5	*For candidates who write about Glasgow, possible answers might include:* • Bypass/ring road: In Glasgow, the M74, M77 or Glasgow Southern Orbital Route mean that through traffic does not need to travel into the city centre **(1 mark)**. • Pedestrianised area in centre: Sections of Argyle Street and Buchanan Street were pedestrianised, the main shopping streets are no longer congested to make it safer and more pleasant for shoppers **(1 mark)**. • Park and ride and improvements to public transport: Commuters have been encouraged to travel into the city centre by train, underground or bus to reduce the number of cars on the road **(1 mark)**. Additional parking has been provided at suburban train stations, eg Hamilton West and Carluke, and new railway stations have opened, eg Larkhall **(1 mark)**. The introduction of bus lanes has reduced journey times along main commuter routes, therefore encouraging people to travel by bus **(1 mark)**. • One way streets: To improve the flow of traffic, the streets around George Square and Hope Street are now one way **(1 mark)**. • Parking restrictions and fines: Parking charges have been increased (60p for 12 minutes in the city centre, with a maximum stay of 2 hours) and traffic wardens patrol the streets to discourage people from bringing their cars into the centre (£60 fines are issued as necessary) **(1 mark)**. • Multi-storey car parks: Multi-storey car parks have been built, eg Buchanan Galleries, to reduce the number of cars parking on the surrounding streets **(1 mark)**. • Bridges and tunnels: Bridges like the Clyde Arc ('Squinty Bridge') and the Clyde Tunnel have been built to improve the flow of traffic from the north to the south of the city, diverting from the CBD thus reducing congestion **(1 mark)**.
6.	Answers will depend on the case study referenced by the candidate. Marks may be awarded as follows: For 1 mark, candidates should briefly describe a strategy and offer one evaluative point. Further developed/detailed evaluative comments should be awarded 1 mark each. At least two strategies are required for full credit. A maximum of 3 marks should be awarded for answers consisting entirely of limited evaluative points. Up to 2 marks can be awarded for description or explanation of strategies (i.e. no evaluation), with two such points required for 1 mark. Credit any other valid responses.	5	*Possible answers might include:* • **Large scale redevelopment:** The Dharavi Redevelopment Project where local people will be moved to high rise apartment blocks, however, only those who have been resident in Dharavi since 2000 will be eligible to move into these apartments **(1 mark)**. Other residents will be moved to other parts of the city, which will break up communities and may result in people being too far from their work **(1 mark)**. The new flats will also be too small for those who currently have workshops above their homes **(1 mark)**. • **Slum Rehabilitation:** has planned and managed improvements such as upgrading mains sewerage to help reduce diseases such as cholera however, within 12 years, only 15% of Dharavi was redeveloped **(1 mark)**. • **Local projects:** Self-help schemes support the efforts of local people to improve their housing, for example by adding an additional floor to buildings thus reducing overcrowding **(1 mark)**. Toilets have been added and are shared by two or three families who help to keep them clean, which has reduced the incidence of water related diseases **(1 mark)**.

Section 3: Global Issues

Question		General marking principle for this type of question	Max mark	Specific marking instruction for this question
7.	(a)	1 mark should be awarded for each detailed explanation. Award a maximum of 4 marks if only human or physical factors are explained (although a physical factor could be linked to a human issue, for example narrow cross section which would reduce the cost). A maximum of 2 marks should be awarded for answers consisting entirely of limited descriptive points, with two such points required for 1 mark. Credit any other valid responses.	5	Narrow cross section of the valley is required in order to reduce construction costs of the dam **(1 mark)**. A deep valley is required behind the dam as this will result in a smaller surface area for the reservoir, thereby reduce loss from evaporation **(1 mark)**. A site which has impermeable rock would be advantageous as this would reduce loss from the reservoir by percolation **(1 mark)**. A site which is close to construction materials would help to reduce the cost of transporting these materials to the construction site **(1 mark)**. An area free from earthquakes or subsidence is needed as the area needs to be able to support the weight of a large dam **(1 mark)**. A site close to areas of farmland or urban areas would help to reduce water/electrical loss during transportation **(1 mark)**. The costs involved in moving people who live in the area to be flooded, to reduce costs for compensation and re-housing **(1 mark)**. The land which is to be flooded should not be valuable, for example high quality farmland or of historic/environmental importance **(1 mark)**. An area with plentiful supply of snowmelt/rainfall/river water is required to ensure a consistently high volume of water in the reservoir **(1 mark)**.
	(b)	Award 1 mark for each detailed explanation. Candidate answers must include both social and economic consequences. No marks should be awarded for negative impacts. Award a maximum of 4 marks if the answer does not clearly relate to a specific named water management project. A maximum of 2 marks should be awarded for answers consisting entirely of limited descriptive points, with two such points required for 1 mark. Credit any other valid responses.	5	*Answers will depend on the water management project chosen but for the Aswan High Dam, possible answers might include:* • Increased access to clean drinking water reduces water borne diseases such as typhoid **(1 mark)**. • Increased irrigation, (with 33,600km² of irrigated land) which allows for two crops a year to be grown, reducing malnutrition **(1 mark)** production of wheat and sugar cane tripled allowing more export crops to be produced **(1 mark)**. • Increase in hydroelectric power (from the 12 generating units in the Dam, these generate approx. 2.1 gigawatts) attracting industries such as smelting industries **(1 mark)**. • The introduction of the Nile perch and tiger fish into Lake Nasser has increased the commercial fishing industry and fishing tourism industry **(1 mark)**. • Industries which require large amounts of water have grown up near to Aswan, for example the Egyptian chemical industry KIMA which makes fertilisers **(1 mark)**.
8.	(a)	1 mark should be awarded for each detailed comparison, or a comparison with a short explanation. A detailed comparison will contain a qualitative statement such as dramatically higher and be supported by the statistics. A maximum of 2 marks should be awarded for answers which are purely descriptive and do not go beyond making comparisons directly from the table, with two such comparisons required for 1 mark. Where candidates refer only to the headings (i.e. not to the data), a maximum of 1 mark should be awarded. Markers should take care to look for comparisons wherever they occur in a candidate's answer. Credit any other valid responses.	4	GDP per person shows that Brazil, Mexico and Cuba are emergent developing countries with an intermediate level of income, while Kenya and Malawi are still classed as low income developing countries **(1 mark)**. Employment in agriculture is far higher in Malawi (90%) than Brazil at 16% so it is less industrialised **(1 mark)**. Adult literacy is far higher in Brazil, Mexico and Cuba than in Malawi suggesting they have more schools **(1 mark)**. Birth rate shows a vast difference in development with both African countries having high birth rates (Kenya – 30%); compared with Mexico at 18%, suggesting lack of contraception/education **(1 mark)**. There is also a large difference between the country with the poorest life – Malawi has a life expectancy of 53 whereas Cuba is 78, suggesting better health care **(1 mark)**.

Question	General marking principle for this type of question	Max mark	Specific marking instruction for this question
(b)	1 mark should be awarded for each detailed explanation, or for two more straightforward explanations A maximum of 2 marks should be awarded for four straightforward descriptive lists exemplified by country name, eg Nigeria can sell oil to make money. There is no need to mention the countries in the question and other countries can be used to exemplify points made. Credit any other valid responses.	6	Some countries have natural resources such as oil, which can be sold to generate foreign currency (**1 mark**). Some countries, eg Chad are landlocked, and find it more expensive to export and import goods (**1 mark**). Countries with a poor education system have many low-skilled workers and are unable to attract foreign investment (**1 mark**). Countries with fertile soils and a suitable climate can grow cash crops which can be sold for income (**1 mark**). Corruption in government such as in Nigeria can lead to money being used inappropriately (**1 mark**). Where countries suffer from conflict or civil war they are unable to keep the economy working and spend extra finance on weapons (**1 mark**). Countries which have accumulated large debts have to repay loans and interest causing less money for services (**1 mark**). Famine can lead to malnutrition, and a reduced capacity to work and create income (**1 mark**).
9. (a)	No marks should be awarded for naming the greenhouse gases as these are included in the diagram. No marks should be awarded for explanations of the enhanced greenhouse effect as this is included in the diagram. 1 mark should be awarded for each detailed explanation, or for two undeveloped points. Undeveloped points may include comparative potency of each gas, or limited reasons for increase. Markers should take care not to credit the same reason twice, eg car ownership. Credit any other valid responses.	4	*Possible answers might include:* The Enhanced Greenhouse effect has been caused by an increase in greenhouse gases within the atmosphere. **Carbon dioxide (remains in the atmosphere for 100 years):** • Burning fossil fuels, for example coal, oil and natural gas release carbon dioxide into the atmosphere, which will trap heat. Coal has been used increasingly to power factories, generate electricity in power stations and to heat homes (**1 mark**). • Increased car ownership has resulted in more petrol and diesel being used to fuel cars (**1 mark**). • Deforestation, especially in the Amazon Rainforest, has resulted in less carbon dioxide being absorbed, and the burning releases more CO_2 (**1 mark**). • Peat bog reclamation (particularly in Scotland and Ireland) during, for example, the construction of wind farms, has also resulted in additional carbon dioxide being released into the atmosphere (**1 mark**). **Methane:** (More than 20 times as effective in trapping heat than CO_2; accounts for 20% of the enhanced greenhouse effect; remains in the atmosphere for 11–12 years) (**1 mark**). • Methane has been released from landfill sites as waste decomposes and when drilling for natural gas (**1 mark**). • The increase in padi fields to feed rapidly growing populations in Asian countries has increased the amount of methane in the atmosphere (**1 mark**). • The increasing demand for beef has resulted in more methane being created by belching cattle and from animal dung (**1 mark**). **Nitrous oxide:** • Nitrous oxide is 200–300 times more effective in trapping heat than carbon dioxide. Increased car exhaust emissions have resulted in more nitrous oxide (**1 mark**). • Due to rising food demand the increased production of fertilisers also adds to the amount of nitrous oxide in the atmosphere (**1 mark**).

Question		General marking principle for this type of question	Max mark	Specific marking instruction for this question
9.	(a)	*(continued)*		**Chlorofluorocarbons (CFCs):** • Refrigerators which are not disposed of correctly release CFCs when the foam insulation inside them is shredded **(1 mark)**. • Air conditioning — the coolants used in air conditioning systems create CFCs, which must be disposed of correctly **(1 mark)**. Credit any relevant developed points.
	(b)	For 1 mark, candidates should give one detailed explanation, or a limited description/explanation of two factors. A maximum of 3 marks should be awarded for answers consisting entirely of limited descriptive points, with two such points required for 1 mark. A maximum of 2 marks should be awarded for answers consist of limited description with a specific example. 1 mark can be awarded where candidates refer to **two** specific named examples accurately linked with an effect (species, ocean currents, or use of figures). Candidates should be credited for both positive and negative effects. Credit any other valid responses.	6	*Possible answers might include:* **Global Effects:** • Sea level rises caused by an expansion of the sea as it becomes warmer and also by the melting of glaciers and ice caps in Greenland, Antarctica, etc. **(1 mark)**. • Low-lying coastal areas, eg Bangladesh affected with large-scale displacement of people and loss of land for farming and destruction of property **(1 mark)**. • More extreme and more variable weather, including floods, droughts, hurricanes, tornadoes becoming more frequent and intense **(1 mark)**. • Globally, an increase in precipitation, particularly in the winter in northern countries such as Scotland, but some areas like the USA Great Plains may experience drier conditions **(1 mark)**. • Increase in extent of tropical/vector borne diseases, eg yellow fever as warmer areas expand, possibly up to 40 million more in Africa being exposed to risk of contracting malaria **(1 mark)**. • Longer growing seasons in many areas in northern Europe for example, increasing food production and range of crops being grown **(1 mark)**. • Impact on wildlife and natural habitats, eg extinction of at least 10% of land species and coral reefs suffer 80% bleaching **(1 mark)**. • Changes to ocean current circulation, eg in the Atlantic the thermohaline circulation starts to lose impact on north-western Europe, resulting in considerably colder winters **(1 mark)**. • Changes in atmospheric patterns linking to changes in the monsoon caused by El Niño, La Niña **(1 mark)**. • Increased risk of forest fires, for example in Australia and California due to change in surface temperatures and changes in rainfall patterns **(1 mark)**.
10.	(a)	Candidates should refer to both social and economic impacts for full credit, although markers should be aware that many impacts could be considered both social and economic. 1 mark should be awarded for each detailed explanation. A maximum of 3 marks should be awarded for answers consisting entirely of limited points, with two such points required for 1 mark. A developed point may be a detailed explanation of an impact, or may be two less detailed impacts. Candidates may choose to answer a mixture of two styles. Credit any other valid responses.	4	*Possible answers might include:* • Economic impacts include many people being trapped in poverty and trying to survive on very little money. This might be because companies in the developed world want to manufacture their product for the cheapest price possible **(1 mark)**. • Many countries are unable to make a decent profit on the goods they sell because they are forced to pay tariffs to "developed countries" in trading blocs **(1 mark)**. • Government subsidies and grants in "developed countries" allow companies to sell products (eg rice and grain) at a cheaper price than is possible in many "developing countries" — undercutting local farmers and causing them to lose money **(1 mark)**. • Social impacts of this poverty include many children working instead of going to school, and this causes an illiterate population, with the consequent lack of opportunities and poorer quality of living for people that this applies to **(1 mark)**.

Question		General marking principle for this type of question	Max mark	Specific marking instruction for this question
10.	(a)	*(continued)*		• Creates a self-perpetuating cycle of poverty where the next generation are unable to access well-paid employment due to being illiterate **(1 mark)**. • The lack of well-paid jobs means many people live in shanty town type accommodation, with little access to clean water, safe electricity, sanitation, etc. **(1 mark)**.
	(b)	1 mark should be awarded for each developed point. A maximum of 4 marks should be awarded for answers consisting entirely of limited points, with two such points required for 1 mark. A developed point may be a detailed explanation or a description of a trend with a less detailed explanation or may be two less detailed explanations. Credit any other valid responses.	6	*Possible answers might include:* • The graph shows that the price of normal coffee is very variable — for example, when there was a drought in Brazil, the global production decreased and so the price of coffee increased **(1 mark)**. • When China and India increased demand this increased competition for coffee and caused the price to increase **(1 mark)**. • When the production of coffee increased this eased competition for coffee and caused the price to drop **(1 mark)**. • In all these cases, fair trade matched any price increases, but also never dropped below 125 cents per kilo. This allows farmers benefiting from fair trade to have security for the future and to make plans to improve their quality of life **(1 mark)**. • Fair Trade Coffee also does not lose money to the extra "links" in the chain that normal coffee has. Each link in the chain (for example, the "middle men" companies), demand a fee and take money away from the farmer. This leaves the farmer with almost nothing to show for growing the coffee in the first place **(1 mark)**. • Fair trade also ensures that the environment of the coffee plantations is not misused and damaged for future generations by farming in a sustainable way **(1 mark)**. • Fair trade also ensures that there are no child workers, so that children get the chance to attend school and improve their opportunities in the future **(1 mark)**. • Fair trade not only benefits the individual farmers, as there are community improvement payments to villages supplying fair trade coffee beans. This allows, for example, new schools and health centres to be built and staffed that would otherwise not have been built **(1 mark)**.
11.	(a)	1 mark should be awarded for each developed point for energy production or for two undeveloped points. A developed point may include a descriptive statistic/comparative statement with explanation or a developed explanation. Where candidates have only described the data, award a maximum of 1 mark. One mark should be awarded for two descriptive points. Credit any other valid responses.	4	*Possible answers might include:* • Saudi Arabia gets 100% of its energy from fossil fuels because it has vast natural resources of oil and gas in its territory **(1 mark)**. • Portugal has the largest amount of other renewables because its climate is sunny, with many cloud-free days for solar power **(1 mark)** and windy with mid-latitude westerly winds blowing over Atlantic Ocean to Portugal for wind power **(1 mark)**. • France has the largest amount of nuclear energy because it has no oil or gas reserves and has used up most of its coal reserves **(1 mark)**. France used to import oil and gas, but started to develop its own nuclear power in a big way after the "oil shock" — when OPEC countries suddenly decided to quadruple the price for oil in 1973 **(1 mark)**. • Paraguay has the largest amount of hydroelectric power because it has large amounts of tropical precipitation and major rivers that can be harnessed **(1 mark)**. • Iceland has the largest amount of geothermal energy because it is located at a plate boundary where the heat of magma is closer to the surface and so can be harnessed efficiently **(1 mark)**.

Question	General marking principle for this type of question	Max mark	Specific marking instruction for this question
(b)	1 mark should be awarded for each developed explanatory point or for two undeveloped points. Take care not to credit reverse statements (for example renewable sources do not pollute and non-renewable sources pollute). Maximum of 4 marks for one energy source. Credit any other valid responses.	6	*Possible answers for all renewable energy sources might include:* • It harnesses a free resource, which is sustainable for the future **(1 mark)**. It does not contribute greenhouse gases such as CO_2 or other pollution in to the atmosphere **(1 mark)**. **Also, for:** • Wind power can be very effective if sited properly in an exposed area where there is regular wind flow to turn the blades **(1 mark)**. A large are of open land is required, close to large cities, for both wind and solar to avoid loss when transporting **(1 mark)**. However, when the wind is not blowing the turbines cannot generate any energy, and at present it is very difficult to store wind power to use when demand needs it **(1 mark)**. Wind turbines built on peat bogs require the bogs to be drained — which releases carbon dioxide that would otherwise have been stored — causing pollution **(1 mark)**. • Solar power is effective on clear, sunny days but is far less effective when clouds block direct sunlight **(1 mark)**. Solar power can be stored in batteries and used at times of high demand **(1 mark)**. Photostatic panels and solar panels have a very high initial cost **(1 mark)**. • Hydroelectric power can be generated as required and so is able to cope with peaks and troughs in demand **(1 mark)**. • Geothermal power can be generated as required and so is able to cope with peaks and troughs in demand **(1 mark)**. It is most effective in areas close to plate boundaries where the heat source underground (magma) is closer to the surface **(1 mark)**. • Tidal power has the potential to generate vast quantities of energy, for example experimental tidal generators in the Pentland Firth **(1 mark)**. Tidal power, unlike wind/solar is predictable, therefore reliable **(1 mark)**. • Technology for wave power, is not yet sufficiently advanced to allow for large scale economic production **(1 mark)**. *Possible answers for all non-renewable energy sources might include:* It can generate power as required and so is able to cope with peaks and troughs in demand **(1 mark)**. However, it harnesses a resource, which will eventually run out and then will effectively be gone for good, so is not a viable long-term energy solution **(1 mark)**. Coal, gas and oil contribute towards global warming and cause air pollution **(1 mark)**. **Also for:** • Coal/gas are a relatively cheap way for a country to generate energy. They can also be moved about relatively easily to where power is being generated **(1 mark)**. • Gas causes less pollution than burning coal (up to 45% less) or oil (up to 30% less) **(1 mark)**.

Question		General marking principle for this type of question	Max mark	Specific marking instruction for this question
11.	(b)	*(continued)*		• Nuclear — due to small amounts of radioactive material needed to produce huge amounts of energy resources will last longer **(1 mark)**. Nuclear power does not produce greenhouse gases, such as CO_2 or other forms of air pollution **(1 mark)**. However, it does produce nuclear waste, which is toxic and needs to be carefully stored for hundreds of thousands of years **(1 mark)**. Also, nuclear reactors are expensive to build and run so are not suitable for all countries **(1 mark)**. A radioactive leak could be devastating for the local people and environment and for future generations **(1 mark)**. • Technology in many developed countries is geared towards non-renewable sources as power stations/infrastructure are already in place **(1 mark)**. • Supply of oil may be disrupted and process rise due to sabotage during wars **(1 mark)**.
12.		Candidates should make reference to all sources, including the OS map to discuss the suitability and impact of the centre. 1 mark should be awarded for each developed explanatory point. 1 mark should be awarded where candidates refer to the resource and offer a brief explanation of its significance (beyond the wording of the resource), or give a limited description/explanation of two factors. A maximum of 5 marks should be awarded for answers consisting entirely of limited descriptive points, with two such points required for 1 mark. A maximum of 4 marks should be awarded for candidates who give vague over-generalised answers, which make no reference to the map. There are a variety of ways for candidates to give map evidence including descriptions, grid references and place names. It is possible that some points referred to as a disadvantage may be interpreted by other candidates as a negative impact. Markers should take care to credit each point only once, where it is best explained.	10	*For suitability, possible answers may include the following positive observations:* **Possible advantages of this location** The surrounding area offers potential for a range of activities such as hillwalking, with steep slopes posing a challenge for mountain biking eg Auchenroy Hill **(1 mark)**, there are numerous trails in nearby woodland which could be used for orienteering eg Galloway Forest Park 488038 **(1 mark)**. Steep, sheer cliffs in the disused quarry at 457054 could be used for abseiling/climbing **(1 mark)**. There are a number of opportunities for watersports such as the River Doon could be used for fishing, or the River Doon and Bogton Loch/Loch Doon could be used for kayaking **(1 mark)**. Local schools at 477060 may be interested in using the facilities for outdoor learning and enriching the curriculum. The SSSI at Bogton Loch and the Nature Reserve at Dalmellington Moss would offer opportunities for exploring the wildlife present **(1 mark)**. Variety of attractive scenery including Dalcairnie Linn waterfall offering potential for geography studies (as per spec) at 467043 **(1 mark)**. There are a number of tourist facilities already in the area (Industrial Railway Centre, horse riding, fishing), and these could work together with the new facility to join up and benefit from each other's custom **(1 mark)**. The centre would be only 0.5 km from the A713 main road and there is access to the site at present, with the B741 to the west and a minor road lying to the east **(1 mark)**. **Possible disadvantages of this location** Large area of marsh/poorly drained land close to the site would present major construction difficulties and could result in expensive remediation work **(1 mark)**. There could be a serious threat of flooding from the loch overflowing after heavy precipitation **(1 mark)**. **Positive impacts** Creation of jobs during construction and in running the centre would be welcome in East Ayrshire where unemployment is about 1—2% above the national average, as shown in Table Q12 **(1 mark)**.

Question	General marking principle for this type of question	Max mark	Specific marking instruction for this question
12.	*(continued)*		This could boost the local economy by attracting more visitors because East Ayrshire at 18% has the lowest income from tourism in Ayrshire and Arran, as shown in Diagram Q12(b) **(1 mark)**. This could help to reverse rural depopulation in the area, as Diagram Q12(a) shows that there was a decrease of about 1,000 people in Dalmellington and Burnton between 2001 and 2010 **(1 mark)**.
			Negative impacts Construction work and the various activities could be very damaging to the fragile environment and could face strong opposition from conservationists **(1 mark)**. The centre and associated infrastructure could spoil the views as it is on flat land, very visible from the road **(1 mark)** and there may be increased air and noise pollution traffic to the area harming the fragile ecosystems in the SSSI **(1 mark)**. Increased litter could lead to farm animals being harmed which could mean a financial loss for nearby farmers — Craigengillan Home Farm 475038 **(1 mark)**.

HIGHER GEOGRAPHY
2016

Section 1: Physical Environments

Question			General marking principle for this type of question	Max mark	Specific marking instructions for this question
1.	(a)(b)		1 mark should be awarded for each developed comparison, or two limited comparisons up to a maximum of 3 marks. For full marks, candidates must answer both parts of the question. Award **1 mark for each detailed explanation or for two limited explanations.** Candidates may choose to answer this question holistically and should be credited accordingly. Award 1 mark for a limited comparison with a limited explanation. Credit any other valid responses	5	**Comparison** should highlight the marked contrast in precipitation totals, seasonal distribution and number of rain days. Figures may provide detail for a comparison, however they are not required. *Answers may include*: Agadez has 200mm rainfall compared with Lagos 1600mm. Agadez has a peak in August, whereas at Lagos there is a higher peak June. **(1 mark)** Agadez has a distinct dry season from October to May with one peak, whereas Lagos has year round rainfall with 2 peaks. **(1 mark)** **Explanation** should focus on explaining the migration of the ITCZ and the movement of the Maritime Tropical and Continental Tropical air masses over the course of the year. *Answers may include*: Lagos sits south of the ITCZ and is influenced by hot, humid maritime tropical air from the Gulf of Guinea for most of the year **(1 mark)**. The twin precipitation peaks can be attributed to the ITCZ moving northwards in the early part of the year and then southwards later in the year in line with thermal equator/overhead sun **(1 mark)**. Agadez, on the other hand, is under the influence of hot, dry continental tropical air blowing from the Sahara and lies well to the north of the ITCZ for most of the year **(1 mark)**.
2.	(a)		1 mark should be awarded for each developed explanation, or for two limited descriptions/explanations. If candidates discuss more than one glaciated area, mark all and award marks to the highest scoring section. If candidates discuss a coastal area, bracket the name off, and award marks to any conflict/strategy which could apply to a glaciated area. Bracket off responses referring to social/economic conflicts, although be aware that candidates may develop this by referring to economic consequences. Credit any other valid responses.	5	Precise points will depend on the conflict and area chosen (although the extracts refers to tourism, note that the question is open to all environmental conflicts). Traffic congestion on narrow rural roads leads to high levels of air and noise pollution **(1 mark)**. Tourists parking on grass verges in honeypot locations such as Bowness can lead to erosion of fragile grass verges **(1 mark)**. Tourists wander off footpaths widening them and stone wall can be damaged by people climbing over them **(1 mark)**. Litter causes visual pollution and can harm wildlife (or livestock) if it is eaten **(1 mark)**. Speedboats on lakes produce oil pollution and can erode beaches **(1 mark)**. Quarrying such as Honister Quarry in the Lake District can produce large quantities of dust which can settle on plants stunting their growth **(1 mark)**. Large lorries travelling to and from the quarries can cause structural damage due to vibrations from the heavily loaded vehicles **(1 mark)**.

Question			General marking principle for this type of question	Max mark	Specific marking instructions for this question
	(b)	(i) (ii)	1 mark should be awarded for each developed explanation and each developed evaluation, or for two limited descriptions/explanations/evaluations. Award 1 mark for a limited explanation with a limited evaluation. Candidates should be awarded a maximum of 4 marks if there is no evaluation. Candidates may choose to answer this question holistically and should be credited accordingly.	5	Removing litter bins in remote areas where it is difficult to empty them (leading to overflowing bins), encourages people to take their litter home (**1 mark**). Traffic restrictions such as one way streets and limited waiting times have had limited success as people prefer the convenience of their own vehicles (**1 mark**). Using farmers' fields as temporary car parks reduces on-street parking and can bring in another form of income for the farmer (**1 mark**). Hosing lorries or covering with tarpaulin has reduced the amount of dust, and transporting by train takes lorries off the road (**1 mark**). Planting trees around unsightly developments can shield them, but this is a long term solution (**1 mark**). New developments are controlled by NPA by-laws ensuring they use local materials which blend in with the landscape (**1 mark**). Speed limits to reduce beach erosion have been implemented, however, this has resulted in speedboat users moving to other lakes (**1 mark**).

Section 2: Human Environments

Question		General marking principle for this type of question	Max mark	Specific marking instructions for this question
3.	(a) (b)	Answers will depend on the case study referenced by the candidate. For full marks candidates must answer both parts of the question. Marks may be awarded as follows: For 1 mark, candidates may give one detailed explanation, or a limited description/explanation of two factors. For 1 mark, candidates may give a developed comment on effectiveness or two limited comments on effectiveness. For 1 mark, candidates may give one limited explanation with one limited comment on effectiveness. Candidate responses are likely to address the question holistically and marks should be awarded accordingly. Credit any other valid responses.	6	*Suitable methods for Africa might include:* • Afforestation projects reduce wind erosion and prevent soil erosion as the tree roots bind the soil and hold it in place (**1 mark**). • However, the current and anticipated cost of the Great Green Wall project has been heavily criticised; it is out of the reach of most developing nations (**1 mark**). • Fanya juu terraces (popular in Makanya in north-eastern Tanzania) have been made by digging a drainage channel and throwing soil uphill to make a ridge to increase infiltration (**1 mark**). • This low technology approach has been particularly successful. However, maintaining the terraces is very labour intensive (**1 mark**). • In Makanya, maize is grown between the trenches increasing crop yield (from 1.5 tonnes per hectare to 2.4 tonnes per hectare) which reduces the need to cultivate more marginal farmland (**1 mark**). • Diguettes or "Magic Stones" are lines of stones placed along the contours of gently sloping land to trap rain water as well as soil (**1 mark**). • This is particularly useful following the seasonal rainfall in the Sahel caused by the ITCZ which causes surface run-off (**1 mark**). • By preserving the most fertile top-soil, stone lines have increased yields by 40% in some areas (**1 mark**).

Question		General marking principle for this type of question	Max mark	Specific marking instructions for this question
		(continued)		• Zai (microbasins, or planting pits) are hollows dug to retain moisture and nutrients **(1 mark)**. • This ensures year round plant coverage which increases infiltration and reduced run-off **(1 mark)**. *Other methods may include:* • Microdams • Education programmes • Managed grazing/moveable fencing *NB Suitable methods for a rainforest area may include:* • Re afforestation • Increased global co-operation • Crop rotation • Agroforestry • National Parks
4.	(a)	For 1 mark, candidates may give one detailed explanation, or a limited description/explanation of two factors. Credit any other valid responses.	3	*Population data can be gathered by:* • Census is a survey carried out every ten years to gather population data **(1 mark)**. • Census: Each householder is asked to complete a detailed questionnaire about the number of people living in their home, their age, gender, employment, home and languages spoken **(1 mark)**. • Civil registrations of births, marriages and deaths keep an up-to-date count of the population **(1 mark)**. • Sampling: Population surveys are conducted to gather social and economic data, and can be conducted at regional, national or international levels **(1 mark)**. • In China National Population Sample Surveys have been conducted annually, with 1% of the population being asked to complete the form **(1 mark)**. • Government records: Information on migration may be gathered from visa applications or Borders Agency **(1 mark)**. • Data from electoral roll and NHS records allows population data to be updated in between census collection **(1 mark)**.
	(b)	Candidates must explain the problems of collecting accurate population data in developing countries. For 1 mark, candidates may give one detailed explanation, or a limited explanation of two factors. Named examples will enhance a candidate's answer, however, a name alone will not gain any credit. Credit any other valid responses.	6	*Problems of gathering population data:* • Language barriers: countries with many official languages have to translate their census forms and employ enumerators who can speak multiple languages **(1 mark)**. • Literacy levels: many people can't read and write, and therefore are unable to complete the forms, or might make mistakes unintentionally **(1 mark)**. • Size of the population: the sheer size of some populations make it very difficult to conduct a census, eg in China and India **(1 mark)**. • Inaccessibility: the poor infrastructure and difficult terrain, for example in the Amazon Rainforest, may make it difficult for enumerators to distribute census forms **(1 mark)**. • Wars/civil wars: conflict can make it too dangerous for enumerators to enter, or for data to quickly become dated **(1 mark)**. • Cost: undertaking the census is a very expensive process, even for developed world countries. In developing countries, there may be higher priorities for spending, including housing, education and health care **(1 mark)**.

Question	General marking principle for this type of question	Max mark	Specific marking instructions for this question
	(continued)		• Migration: rapid rural to urban migration can make it difficult to gather accurate population data as data will become outdated very quickly **(1 mark)**. • Many people in developing countries may be living in shanty towns, eg Dhararvi, or are homeless, so have no official address making it difficult to count them **(1 mark)**. • People who are illegal immigrants are unlikely to complete a census for fear of deportation, leading to inaccurate data **(1 mark)**. • Nomadic people: large numbers of migrants, eg the Tuareg, Fulani or Bedouin, or shifting cultivators in the Amazon can easily be missed or counted twice **(1 mark)**. • Ethnic tensions and internal political rivalries may lead to inaccuracies, eg northern Nigeria was reported to have inflated its population figures to secure increased political representation **(1 mark)**.

Section 3: Global Issues

Question		General marking principle for this type of question	Max mark	Specific marking instructions for this question
5.	(a)	1 mark should be awarded for a detailed explanation or a limited description/ explanation of two factors; this may include the use of facts from the resources. Credit any other valid responses.	6	• Population increase of almost 50 million for country in last 20 years would require additional water for domestic use **(1 mark)**. • Irrigation is required for rice production to feed the population or for export **(1 mark)**. • Textile industries use large volumes of water therefore a reliable year round supply is required **(1 mark)**. • Due to the monsoon climate a lack of rainfall in Nov–March increases the need for water to be stored to allow use during the dry period **(1 mark)**. • The heavy monsoon rainfall of up to 800mm of rain in the month of July means there is a requirement to prevent flooding **(1 mark)**. • The city of Chittagong has a population of 7.5 million and is situated on the banks of the river; this increases the need for flood prevention **(1 mark)**. • Only 62% of the country has access to electricity, HEP from the dam could be used to improve this **(1 mark)**. • Excess energy produced could be exported to neighbouring countries such as India **(1 mark)**. • Improved sanitation means that far less of the population will be at risk from diseases such as cholera **(1 mark)**.
	(b)	Answers must discuss the possible positive **and** negative **environmental** impacts. Award a maximum of 3 marks for either. 1 mark should be awarded for a developed explanation, or a more straightforward explanation linked to the case study. Care should be taken not to credit purely social or economic benefits but markers should be aware that some candidates will be able to link these to the environment. Award a maximum of 3 marks if the answer is vague/does not relate to a specific named water management project.	4	*Answers will depend on the water management project chosen but for the Aswan High Dam, possible answers might include:* • Lake Nasser provides a sanctuary for waterfowl and wading birds and has more than 32 species of fish **(1 mark)**. • River and irrigation water becomes saline with high evaporation rates resulting in farmers downstream having to switch to more salt-tolerant crops **(1 mark)**. • The change in river regime has caused the loss of many animal habitats, eg the drying up of the Nile delta area may lead to inundation of sea water **(1 mark)**.

Question			General marking principle for this type of question	Max mark	Specific marking instructions for this question
	(b)		*(continued)*		• The water table is rising in the Nile valley, which is resulting in major erosion of foundations of ancient temples and monuments such as Abu Simbel **(1 mark)**. • Increase in 'clean' hydro-electric power from the 12 generating units in the Dam, instead of using polluting fossil fuels **(1 mark)**. • The lack of flooding and subsequent lack of silt deposition has led to a need for chemical fertilisers which has resulted in high levels of nitrogen and phosphorous being washed into rivers **(1 mark)**. • The sediments which were transported to the river mouth forming a delta are now trapped behind the dam, a situation which has led to severe erosion along the Egyptian coast **(1 mark)**.
6.	(a)		1 mark should be awarded for each detailed evaluation of the indicator, or for two more straightforward reasons. Candidates may respond by explaining the benefits of composite or other indicators. This should be credited accordingly.	3	• Single indicators such as GNI are averages which can hide extremes within a country such as a rich minority and a poor majority **(1 mark)**. • Development is not only about money, other aspects of development like literacy and health care are also important **(1 mark)**. • Composite indicators such as HDI give a more rounded picture; by combining a number of indicators **(1 mark)**. • It is not possible to tell where a rise in GNI is being spent within a country — not always spent on improving standard of living **(1 mark)**. • GNI is always expressed as US$ to allow comparison, however exchange rates continually fluctuate **(1 mark)**. • GNI does not take into account the informal economy however this accounts for a large proportion of wealth generated in some countries **(1 mark)**.
	(b)	(i) (ii)	1 mark should be awarded for each developed explanation or for two less developed explanations. A developed point may be: • a detailed explanation • a description of a strategy with a less detailed explanation • two less detailed explanations Evaluations may refer to why a strategy is suited to a developing country or by giving data to show how successful a programme has been. Answers which provide no evaluation should be awarded a maximum of 6 marks. Candidates may choose to answer holistically and should be credited accordingly. 1 mark should be awarded for a limited explanation with a limited evaluation. Candidate may discuss malaria in this question; only strategies which could be considered PHC should be credited.	7	• Oral Rehydration Therapy is the mixture of salt and sugar with clean water to help people suffering from diarrhoea **(1 mark)**; it is very effective as it is cheap and simple and it can be administered by untrained staff **(1 mark)**. • Vaccination programmes such as the UNICEF run polio immunisation campaign were delivered to rural areas as people here find it more difficult to access health care **(1 mark)**. • By 2014 polio was endemic in only three countries (Afghanistan, Pakistan and Nigeria) **(1 mark)**. • Charities such as Water Aid work with countries and other aid agencies to improve water and sanitation by installing, eg pit latrines **(1 mark)**. • By 2010 the number of people without access to improved drinking water had decreased to (11%) and the ash compost from latrines can improve crop yield **(1 mark)**. • Barefoot Doctors provide health education through play and songs as many people are illiterate in developing countries **(1 mark)**. • Insecticide treated bed nets provide a physical barrier against the mosquito and kills the mosquito preventing further spread **(1 mark)**. • However, they need to be treated regularly to be effective and in some cases are damaged by being used as fishing nets **(1 mark)**. • Play Pumps International provide roundabouts which extract ground water which can be used for drinking **(1 mark)**. These provide local people with transferable skills and use appropriate level of technology **(1 mark)**.

Question			General marking principle for this type of question	Max mark	Specific marking instructions for this question
7.	(a)		1 mark should be awarded for each detailed explanation or for a limited description/explanation of two factors. Markers should take care not to credit human causes of climate change. Credit any other valid responses.	4	*Possible answers might include:* • Milankovitch's theory: changes in the Earth's orbit and tilt alter the amount of energy reaching the Earth **(1 mark)**. • Every 41,000 years, there is a change in the tilt of the Earth's axis. A greater tilt means more sunlight in polar regions **(1 mark)**. • Over a 97,000 year cycle, the Earth's orbit stretches, affecting the amount of energy received **(1 mark)**. • Sunspot activity: global mean temperatures can be raised by peaks of sunspot activity, which follow an 11-year pattern **(1 mark)**. • Volcanic eruptions: after violent eruptions, large amounts of dust and droplets of sulphur may reflect the Sun's rays lowering temperature **(1 mark)**. • Retreating ice caps release additional fresh water leading to changes in oceanic circulation **(1 mark)**. • This also reduces the albedo effect as reflection has decreased as more land is exposed **(1 mark)**. • Melting permafrost: methane being released from melting permafrost from decomposing organic matter **(1 mark)**.
	(b)		For 1 mark, candidates should give one detailed explanation of the strategies used to manage climate change, or a limited description/explanation of two factors. Candidates do not need to refer to local, national and international strategies to gain full credit. Named examples will enhance a candidate's answer; however, an example alone will not gain any credit. Credit any other valid responses.		**Local—** • Individuals can reduce, re-use and recycle products so that less refuse is sent to landfill sites. This will reduce the amount of methane entering the atmosphere **(1 mark)**. • To reduce the amount of carbon dioxide generated by the burning of fossil fuels, households could reduce energy consumption by insulating their homes or switching lights off, etc. **(1 mark)**. • People could also be encouraged to use public transport, walk or cycle, or use hybrid or electric cars to cut down on fossil fuel consumption **(1 mark)**. • Fridge disposal should be managed carefully to ensure CFC gases don't escape. New cooling units no longer emit CFCs **(1 mark)**. **National—** • Government policies such as 'Helping Households to cut their Energy Bills' encourage the use of 'Smart Meters' improving energy efficiency **(1 mark)**. • Increasing the use of low carbon technologies such as windfarms: the UK Government is committed to creating 15% of energy by renewable sources **(1 mark)**. **International—** • The Paris Agreement outlined agreements between leaders of developed and developing countries to limit climate change below a 2° rise **(1 mark)**. • The European Union has committed to reducing carbon emissions by 20% by 2020. The EU will reward developing countries financially **(1 mark)**. • The impact of climate change could also be managed by preparing for extreme weather events, for example flood defences could be built to hold back flood water, or flood plains and natural wetlands could be used to store flood water **(1 mark)**.

Question		General marking principle for this type of question	Max mark	Specific marking instructions for this question
8.	(a)	1 mark should be awarded for each detailed comparison, or a comparison with a short explanation. A detailed comparison will contain a qualitative statement such as dramatically higher and be supported by the statistics. A maximum of 2 marks should be awarded for answers which are purely descriptive and do not go beyond making comparisons directly from the table, with two such comparisons required for 1 mark. Where candidates refer only to the headings (i.e. not to the data), a maximum of one mark should be awarded. Markers should take care to look for comparisons wherever they occur in a candidate's answer. Credit any other valid responses.	4	*Possible answers might include:* • Some countries can afford to buy in lots of imports (like USA who spend $2,273 billion) whereas other countries cannot afford to (like Zimbabwe who spend $4 billion) **(1 mark)**. • Some countries can sell manufactured goods to make money (for example, China who make $2,210 billion from exports), whereas other countries rely on raw materials (for example, Botswana who make $3 billion from exports) **(1 mark)**. • China has the biggest trade surplus of $438 billion compared to the USA, which has the biggest trade deficit of $698 billion **(1 mark)**. • Two countries with similar population sizes are Australia and Ghana, yet Australia has a trade surplus of $7 billion and a GDP per capita of $67,304, whereas Ghana has a trade deficit of $5 billion and a GDP per capita of $3,500 **(1 mark)**. • Two countries with similar population sizes are China and India, yet China has a trade surplus of $438 billion and a GDP per capita of $6,071, whereas India has a trade deficit of $198 billion and a GDP per capita of $1,499 **(1 mark)**.
	(b)	1 mark should be awarded for each detailed explanation, or for two more straightforward explanations. A maximum of 2 marks should be awarded for four straightforward descriptive lists, exemplified by country names. Take care not to credit the reverse points of answers with regards to primary/ manufactured products. Credit any other valid responses.	6	*Possible answers might include:* • Some countries have the knowledge and technology to make and sell manufactured products, which sell at high prices and so larger profits are made **(1 mark)**. • These manufactured products sell for a more stable price so countries can plan for the future with confidence in future income **(1 mark)**. • These primary products sell for prices that fluctuate, and so countries cannot invest in development for the future **(1 mark)**. • Often it is the 'developed countries', which set the price for primary products and keep them as low as possible by playing 'developing countries' against each other **(1 mark)**. • Some countries are too reliant on one or two low value exports, and so if anything happens to the price/production of these export products, the country's economy is hit badly **(1 mark)**. • For example, Saudi Arabia exports oil which is in high demand, whereas Burkina Faso exports shea nuts **(1 mark)**. • Trading blocs (like the EU) can control the trade terms for the benefit of its members and make it difficult for non-members to do as well **(1 mark)**. For example, they can set up tariffs and import duties that they charge non-member countries, which makes their goods appear less competitive **(1 mark)**. • They can also set quotas, which put a limit on the amount of product that a non-member country can sell to the member country **(1 mark)**.

Question			General marking principle for this type of question	Max mark	Specific marking instructions for this question
9.	(a)		1 mark should be awarded for each developed point or for two less developed points. A developed point may be a detailed explanation or a description of a trend with a less detailed explanation or may be two less detailed explanations. Credit any other valid responses.	5	• Increased vehicle ownership due to two-car households therefore increased demand for petrol **(1 mark)**. • Increased ownership of electronic devices such as tablets, due to changing technology and affordability therefore increased demand for electricity **(1 mark)**. • Increased standard of living and more single occupancy households leading to more houses with central heating systems **(1 mark)**. • Improved energy efficiency in residential sector: for example, energy-saving fridges and LED lighting **(1 mark)**. • Improved insulation of housing, such as cavity wall insulation cuts down on heat loss causing less heating to be required **(1 mark)**. • Improved efficiency in cars and the growth of more affordable fuel efficient, 'greener' hybrid cars **(1 mark)**. • Government initiatives, such as the cycle to work scheme encourage people to leave their cars at home by subsiding the cost of cycle purchase **(1 mark)**. • The Government signed up to the Kyoto Protocol to reduce greenhouse gas emissions. This has led to targets for industry to meet in terms of energy savings **(1 mark)**. • Significant dip around 2008 due to declining industrial output caused by the recession and subsequent lowering of manufacturing industry in the UK **(1 mark)**.
	(b)		Award 1 mark for each developed advantage or disadvantage or for every two undeveloped points. Candidates must discuss advantages and disadvantages to gain full credit. Candidates must discuss a non-renewable source of energy. No marks for discussing renewable sources of energy. Candidates are expected to consider different aspects of their chosen source of energy. Credit any other valid responses.	5	*Possible answers for all non-renewable energy sources might include:* • They provide instant power as required meeting demand at peak times such as early evening **(1 mark)**. • They cause air pollution and release greenhouse gases so contribute towards global warming **(1 mark)**. *For 'fracking' other possible answers might include:* • The shale gas provides an alternative energy source reducing reliance on traditional fossil fuels such as oil which are finite **(1 mark)**. • Noise and light pollution is increased due to 24hr production on shale gas sites **(1 mark)**. • In USA shale gas production has allowed it to become self-sufficient in gas and means it does not have to rely on imports from other countries **(1 mark)**. • However, the fracking fluid used in the process could pollute ground water and enter the domestic water system **(1 mark)**. • The fracking process could be linked to causing minor earthquakes and tremors in the local area leading to structural damage to buildings and infrastructure **(1 mark)**.

Section 4: Application of Geographical Skills

Question		General marking principle for this type of question	Max mark	Specific marking instructions for this question
10.	(a)	Candidates should make reference to all sources, including the OS map to discuss the suitability and impact of the by-pass route. It is possible that some points referred to as a disadvantage may be interpreted by other candidates as a negative impact. Markers should take care to credit each point only once, where it is best explained. 1 mark should be awarded where candidates refer to the resource and offer a brief explanation of its significance, or give a limited description/explanation of two factors. A maximum of 5 marks should be awarded for answers consisting solely of limited descriptive points with two such points required for 1 mark. A maximum of 4 marks should be awarded for candidates who give vague over-generalised answers, which make no reference to the map. There are a variety of ways for candidates to give map evidence including descriptions, grid references and place names. Credit any other valid responses.	10	*Possible advantages of this route:* • For the first 700m of the route at 745094, the road will be following a dismantled railway line. This will make the road easier to build here, and so reduce costs **(1 mark)**. *Possible disadvantages of this route:* • The new road will require several bridges to be built over rivers and the railway line (774113), which will increase the costs **(1 mark)**. • A road cutting required on approach to Upper Wilting farm as land rises steeply from Combe Haven may require more complex engineering works **(1 mark)**. • The new road crosses an area of marshland in square 7510, which will require costly drainage **(1 mark)**. • The new road is in the flood plain of Watermill Stream/ Combe Haven, and so is at risk of flooding **(1 mark)**. *Possible impacts on the surrounding area might include:* **Negative Environmental Impacts** Diagram Q10C makes it clear that Sussex Wildlife Trust think the road will cause "unacceptable environmental damage". They might be referring to the fact that: • It will require the destruction of deciduous woodland at Chapel Wood and Park Wood (7711), which will cause habitat loss **(1 mark)**. • The road will spoil a natural landscape and cause visual pollution for walkers on the 1066 country walk **(1 mark)**. • The route passes close to sites of conservation value (SSSI, SNCI and an AONB), which could be spoiled by the amount of noise and air pollution a new road will bring **(1 mark)**. • The photograph shows street lighting following the new road which will cause light pollution to a rural area **(1 mark)**. **Positive Environmental Impacts** • Diagram Q10C shows that Glyne Gap is currently suffering from unsafe levels of air pollution on many days (sometimes as many as 16 days in a month), which the by-pass will reduce, improving the air quality here **(1 mark)**. • This will also reduce the noise pollution for local people in this area such as the suburbs of Bexhill, eg Pebsham **(1 mark)**. **Negative Socio-Economic Impacts** • The route passes through or very nearby several farms (Acton's Farm, Adam's Farm, Lower Wilting Farm for example), which could cause the disruption to the farmers as farm animals could be frightened by the noise of vehicles using the new road **(1 mark)**. • The route passes over several footpaths and bridleways including the "1066 Country Walk – Bexhill Link", which might be closed or at least spoiled by a busy new road **(1 mark)**. **Positive Socio-Economic Impacts** • Diagram Q10A shows that the A259 at Glyne Gap is currently very busy all day (with a peak flow of just under 2600 vehicles in an hour). The new road would reduce the traffic flow here dramatically, reducing traffic congestion **(1 mark)**. • This would save journey/commuting time and reduce transport costs for local people/businesses **(1 mark)**. • Building the new road will create many jobs and increase money for people in the local area, which will boost the economy **(1 mark)**.

HIGHER GEOGRAPHY
2017

Section 1: Physical Environments

Question	General marking instructions for this type of question	Max mark	Specific marking instructions for this question
1.	Award a maximum of 4 marks for either feature. Check any diagram(s) for relevant explanations not present in the text and award accordingly. Well-annotated diagrams can gain full marks. Credit an explanation of the formation of glaciers to a maximum of 1 mark. Award a maximum of 1 mark for three or more correctly named, but undeveloped, processes. If a candidate merely explains processes, award a maximum of 2 marks for fully developed processes for any one feature (ie if no reference to the feature). Answers which are purely descriptive, or have no mention of any processes or conditions, should achieve no more than 2 marks (for each feature) in total, with 1 mark being awarded for every two descriptive points being made. **(1 mark)** Limited explanation — the use of the names of at least two processes in context with no development of these. **(2 marks)** The use of the names of at least two processes with development of these, but no other reference to conditions. **OR** Limited use of the names of at least two processes, with at least two descriptive points about the landscape formation. **3 marks** Two developed processes with limited explanation of how the feature forms over time. **4 marks** Two named processes with development of these, with two further statements explaining the formation of the feature.	7	*Glacier formation includes:* • Snow accumulates in north facing hollows when more snow falls in winter than melts in the summer. **(1 mark)** OR • North/north-east facing slopes are more shaded so snow lies longer with accumulated snow compressed into ice. **(1 mark)** *Processes include:* • Plucking, when ice freezes on to bedrock, pulling loose rocks away from the backwall, making it steeper. **(1 mark)** • Abrasion, when the angular rock embedded in the ice grinds the hollow, making it deeper. **(1 mark)** • Frost shattering when water in cracks in the rock freezes, expands and contracts weakening the rock until fragments break off. **(1 mark)** **Corrie:** • Bergschrund crevasse opens up at the back of the hollow. This allows melt-water and rock fragments to get to the base of the glacier increasing abrasion. **(1 mark)** • The weight of the glacier pushes down causing rotational sliding which deepens the hollow. **(1 mark)** • Friction causes the ice to slow down at the front edge of the corrie, allowing a rock lip to form, which traps water as ice melts, leaving a lochan or tarn. **(1 mark)** **U-shaped valleys/hanging valleys:** • The weight of the glaciers causes them to flow downhill following existing V-shaped valleys. **(1 mark)** • Former interlocking spurs may be cut off by the glacier as it flows downhill leaving truncated spurs and steep valley sides. **(1 mark)** • The width and shape of the resulting glacial trough will depend on the nature of the rock type and the intensity and weight of the glacial and it erosion. **(1 mark)** • Tributary valleys have smaller less powerful glaciers which result in less deep U-shaped valleys 'hanging' about the main valley. **(1 mark)** **Terminal moraine:** • Terminal moraine is a ridge across the valley and made up of glacial deposits/till/boulder clay; which is unsorted. **(1 mark)** • As the glacier moves downhill it acts like a bulldozer, pushing sediment in front of its snout as it goes. **(1 mark)** • On reaching lower altitudes and when temperatures rise, the glacier melts, losing power and depositing the moraine. **(1 mark)**

Question			General marking instructions for this type of question	Max mark	Specific marking instructions for this question
			(continued)		• Terminal moraine marks the furthest point that the glacier reaches. Once the ice has retreated, the terminal (or end) moraine can often form a natural dam, creating a ribbon lake. **(1 mark)** **Drumlin:** • Drumlins are elongated hills made up of unsorted glacial deposits/till/boulder clay. **(1 mark)** • Drumlins are formed as the glacier becomes overloaded with sediment and deposits it, streamlining the sediment as it flows over it. **(1 mark)** • The steep 'stoss' slope faces up-valley and the more gently-sloping 'lee' slope faces down-valley. **(1 mark)** • If there is a small obstacle on the ground, this may act as a trigger point and till/boulder clay can build up around it. **(1 mark)** • Drumlins may be reshaped by further ice movements after being originally deposited. Drumlins are found in swarms or in a 'basket of eggs' topography. **(1 mark)** **Esker:** • Eskers are meandering ridges formed by meltwater streams in or underneath a glacier. **(1 mark)** • They are therefore made up of meltwater sands and gravels. These are sorted by size with large stones at the base because larger stones are dropped first by flowing water. **(1 mark)** • The stones also tend to be more rounded than glacial deposits, because of the action of flowing water rounding the edges by erosion. **(1 mark)** • As the glacier melts, sub-glacial streams flow through tunnels and the load is deposited on the channel bed. **(1 mark)** Or any other valid point.
2.			Award 1 mark for each developed explanation or for two less developed explanations. A diagram can be used to add development to a point. Check any diagram(s) for relevant explanations not present in the text and award accordingly. Well-annotated diagrams can gain full marks. Credit any valid responses.	4	*Explanations for the differences between tropical areas and polar areas may include:* • Due to the curve of the Earth the sun's rays are concentrated on a much smaller surface area over the tropical latitudes resulting in more energy. **(1 mark)** • Rays have less atmosphere to pass through at the Tropics so less energy is lost through absorption and reflection. **(1 mark)** • Albedo differs between Tropics and Poles – darker forest surfaces absorb radiation. **(1 mark)** • Lighter snow/ice covered areas at the poles have a higher albedo and reflect more radiation. **(1 mark)** • Due to the tilt of the Earth there is no insolation at the poles during the winter solstices/tropical areas receive insolation all year round. **(1 mark)** Or any other valid point.

Question			General marking instructions for this type of question	Max mark	Specific marking instructions for this question
3.			Well-annotated diagrams that explain conditions and processes can gain full marks. Marks may be awarded as follows: For 1 mark, candidates may give one detailed explanation. For 1 mark, candidates may give a limited description with a limited explanation. A maximum of 2 marks should be awarded for answers consisting entirely of limited descriptive points, with two such points required for 1 mark.	4	• Low temperatures lead to a slow rate of decomposition of organic matter creating a thin humus. **(1 mark)** • Plant roots do not penetrate deeply resulting in limited recycling of minerals back to the vegetation. **(1 mark)** • Anaerobic conditions mean few organisms living in soil to burrow and tunnel through the soil. **(1 mark)** • Soil has a blue grey colour due anaerobic conditions. **(1 mark)** • The iron compounds are changed from red brown to blue due to oxygen being extracted by microorganisms. **(1 mark)** • Red mottling in small air pockets due to re-oxygenation of the iron in the soil due to burrowing animals/soil drying out in summer. **(1 mark)** • Impermeable clay impedes drainage and causes waterlogging. Found on flat surfaces such as plateau moorland or foot of slope means water cannot drain away. **(1 mark)** Or any other valid point.

Section 2: Human Environments

Question			General marking principle for this type of question	Max mark	Specific marking instructions for this question
4.	(a)		For 1 mark, candidates may give one detailed explanation, or a limited description/explanation of two factors. A maximum of 2 marks should be awarded for answers consisting entirely of limited descriptive points, with two such points required for one mark. A maximum of 3 marks should be awarded for either push or pull factors. Where candidates give generic answers which do not refer to a named migration flow, a maximum of 3 marks should be awarded.	4	*For Poland to Scotland:* **Push factors:** • Not enough jobs with very few opportunities for example in 2014 the unemployment rate in Poland was around 14%. **(1 mark)** • Low paying jobs resulting in a low standard of living for example poor quality housing. **(1 mark)** • State benefits are very low compared to Scotland and the UK and also the healthcare in Scotland is free at the point of delivery. **(1 mark)** • Due to increased mechanisation/privatisation of farms rural unemployment has risen. **(1 mark)** **Pull factors:** • Due to Poland joining the European Union, this allowed people to move freely with unlimited migration. **(1 mark)** • The exchange rate meant that the sterling conversion into zloty was favourable and meant that people could send money back to family members in Poland. **(1 mark)** • There were plenty of available jobs in parts of the economy such as in construction and trades such as plumbers and electricians. **(1 mark)** Or any other valid point.
	(b)		For 1 mark, candidates may give one detailed impact, or a limited description/explanation of two impacts. Care should be taken to ensure impacts are relevant to specific case studies and not overly generalised.	3	*For Poland to Scotland voluntary migration:* **Impacts on donor country:** • Fewer people means less pressure on limited resources like good quality housing and healthcare allowing living standards to improve. **(1 mark)**

Question			General marking principle for this type of question	Max mark	Specific marking instructions for this question
			(continued)		• This will also help reduce the unemployment rates for the country and migrants return with new skills. **(1 mark)** • Birth rate is lowered as male migrants are away so there will be a decline in the population further reducing strain on resources. **(1 mark)** • Migrants often send money home to their families meaning people have more money in Poland helping to improve standard of living. **(1 mark)** • The most educated and healthy leave which could hinder development and it tends to be older population that stay behind. **(1 mark)** **Impacts on receiving country:** • The government receives tax from migrant workers who are doing jobs that British people will not do due to low wages and unsociable hours, including fish processing, farm work and cleaning. **(1 mark)** • Generally, migrants are perceived as hard workers and many are highly skilled and/or graduates so brought sought after skills during the UK construction boom. **(1 mark)** • The language barrier and cultural differences can lead to racial tension with ethnic groups tending not to integrate which can add to the tension. **(1 mark)** • May lead to the development of over-crowded, multi occupancy accommodation due to the pressures on housing in certain areas. **(1 mark)** • The education system may become strained due to the number of children for whom English is not their first language. **(1 mark)** • Due to the number of migrants entering Scotland this can lead to increased unemployment rates as a knock-on of the economic downturn. **(1 mark)** • Positives for a multicultural society would include Polish shops or aisles in supermarkets. **(1 mark)** Or any other valid point.
5.			For 1 mark, candidates may give one detailed impact, or a limited description/explanation of two impacts. Care should be taken to ensure impacts are relevant to specific case studies and not overly generalised.	4	*For the Sahel:* • Loss of fertile topsoil leading to the inability of the land to support vegetation. **(1 mark)** • Crop failures/death of livestock, reducing food supply, leading to malnutrition and famine in Sudan, Ethiopia and much of Sahel. **(1 mark)** • Large scale rural migration into overcrowded urban areas in the south, causing more pressure and the growth of shanty towns. **(1 mark)** • The collapse of the nomadic way of life due to the lack of grazing and water forcing many nomads to settle in villages increasing pressure/tension in these areas. **(1 mark)** • Economically, farmers have lost their income as a result of poor crop yields meaning they can no longer afford to pay for their basic needs, such as schooling. **(1 mark)**

Question			General marking principle for this type of question	Max mark	Specific marking instructions for this question
			(continued)		• Conflict within and sometimes, between countries as people are forced to move and re-settle -growth of large refugee camps. **(1 mark)** • Countries increasingly reliant on international aid to gain access to food and water impacting development as debt repayments are high. **(1 mark)** • Desertification has become so severe that it has led to the southward expansion of the Sahara desert into the Sahel. In the last 50 years, 65 million hectares of the Sahel have turned into desert. **(1 mark)** Or any other valid point.
6.			Marks may be awarded as follows: For 1 mark, candidates should briefly describe a strategy and offer one evaluative point. Further developed/detailed evaluative comments should be awarded 1 mark each. 1 mark can be awarded for every two limited evaluative points. At least two strategies are required for full credit. Up to 2 marks can be awarded where candidates only describe or explain strategies (ie no evaluation), with two such points required for one mark. Where candidates give generic answers which do not refer to a city, a maximum of 3 marks should be awarded. If candidates discuss developing world cities, credit any evaluative points which could be relevant to a developed world city, which uses a similar strategy, up to a maximum of 3 marks.	4	*For Glasgow answers may include:* • Pedestrianisation of CBD roads eg Buchanan Street, Argyle Street etc increases pedestrian safety making the areas more appealing for shoppers. **(1 mark)** • Fewer cars in this area leads to lower emissions and improves air quality and environment. **(1 mark)** • Traffic management systems such as one-way streets are used which is successful as they reduce waiting times at junctions. **(1 mark)** • Bus lanes to speed up public transport make it more efficient and so discourage the use of private transport. **(1 mark)** • Improved public transport eg installing free Wi-Fi on buses/trains however many people prefer the convenience of using their own car. **(1 mark)** • Parking restrictions and fines have reduced the amount of on street parking which allows the streets to be wider allowing more space for cars. **(1 mark)** • New links to motorway extensions (M74) to bypass congested areas has removed unnecessary through traffic from bottlenecks such as the Kingston Bridge. **(1 mark)** Or any other valid point.

Section 3: Global Issues

Question			General marking principle for this type of question	Max mark	Specific marking instructions for this question
7.	(a)		1 mark should be awarded for each detailed explanation. A maximum of 2 marks should be awarded for answers consisting entirely of limited descriptive points, with two such points required for one mark. Markers should take care not to credit human factors. Although there could be overlap with factors like cost, this must be clearly linked to the physical environment.	4	• Narrow and deep valleys can be dammed more efficiently and require less construction materials reducing the overall cost of the project, these valleys also have a reduced surface area and combined with low temperatures they reduce water loss from evaporation **(2 marks)** • If the site has impermeable rock this would reduce water loss from the reservoir by percolation. **(1 mark)** • A geologically stable area away from earthquake zones/fault lines with a solid foundation will reduce the risk of damage or failure of the dam. **(1 mark)**

Question			General marking principle for this type of question	Max mark	Specific marking instructions for this question
			(continued)		• A high drainage density (or high rainfall) will ensure that the reservoir will receive enough water to avoid transfer from adjacent drainage basins. **(1 mark)** Or any other valid point.
	(b)		Award 1 mark for each detailed explanation. Candidate answers must include both socio-economic and environmental adverse consequences a maximum of 5 marks should be awarded if only one is discussed. No marks should be awarded for positive impacts. Award a maximum of 5 marks if the answer does not clearly relate to a specific named water management project. A maximum of 3 marks should be awarded for answers consisting entirely of limited descriptive points, with two such points required for one mark.	6	*For the Three Gorges Dam, China, possible answers might include:* **Socio-economic consequences:** • The displacement of millions of people from the Yangtze river region; hundreds of towns and villages were evacuated and later submerged with the area. **(1 mark)** • Those forced to relocate were promised compensation for the value of their homes and land although this did not cover the cost of relocation and some of the money was lost through corruption. **(1 mark)** • Compensation in some instances has been as little as the equivalent of £5 a month, and many claim they have received only half the land compensation they were promised. **(1 mark)** • This has resulted in problems for many as the cities and towns they have had to move to are more expensive, driving many people deeper into poverty. **(1 mark)** • The displaced people are mainly farmers with little formal education this makes it difficult for them to find jobs in the cities and towns they have been relocated to. **(1 mark)** • Flooding the reservoir has forced those farmers still in the region to migrate northwards on to the mountain slopes, adding to erosion. **(1 mark)** **Environmental consequences:** • Construction of the dam has led to an increase in landslides in the area as a result of erosion caused by the increases and decreases in reservoir water. **(1 mark)** • There are 300 species of fish in the Yangtze River. The dam has created a barrier in the river and fish will not be able to travel upstream to spawn, so the populations of the species have decreased. **(1 mark)** • The Chinese River Dolphin is only found in the Yangtze and the construction area covers a large part of this animal's habitat so it is at risk of becoming extinct. **(1 mark)** • Decreases in freshwater flow have meant that more saltwater is creeping up the Yangtze, endangering fish populations already threatened by overfishing. **(1 mark)**
8.	(a) (b)		Candidates may choose to answer parts (a) and (b) separately or together. Award a maximum of 7 marks if there is no comment on effectiveness. Each evaluation should only be credited once – ie candidates should be credited for eg cost only once. Care should be taken not to credit reversals.	10	*Measures taken to eradicate the mosquitoes:* • One method used was to spray pesticides/insecticides in an attempt to kill the Anopheles mosquitoes which spread the disease. **(1 mark)** • Breeding genetically modified sterile mosquitoes (or mosquitoes unable to carry the parasite or mosquitoes which give birth to predominantly male offspring) were also attempts to reduce the numbers of female mosquitoes. **(1 mark)**

Question	General marking principle for this type of question	Max mark	Specific marking instructions for this question
	For 1 mark, candidates should briefly explain a strategy and offer one limited evaluation or one detailed explanation of a strategy or one detailed comment on effectiveness of a strategy. Up to 3 marks can be awarded for description of strategies, with two such points required for 1 mark.		• Another method was to use specially designed mosquito traps, which mimic animals and humans by emitting a small amount of carbon dioxide in order to lure the mosquitoes into the trap where they are killed. **(1 mark)** • BTI bacteria artificially grown in coconuts – the fermented coconuts are broken open after a few days and thrown into the mosquito larvae-infested ponds. The larvae eat the bacteria and have their stomach lining destroyed. **(1 mark)** • Putting larvae-eating fish such as the muddy loach into stagnant ponds or paddi fields can also help to reduce the larvae as the fish eat the larvae. **(1 mark)** • Flushing reservoirs and draining stagnant ponds or swamps every seven days as it takes longer than this period of time for the larvae to develop into adult mosquitoes. **(1 mark)** • Planting eucalyptus trees can help soak up excess moisture and reduce the amount of stagnant water. **(1 mark)** • Covering standing water and water storage cans (eg the Oxfam Bucket) reduces the chances of mosquitoes breeding there. **(1 mark)** *Measures taken to treat those suffering from Malaria include:* • Drugs such as Quinine/Chloroquine/Larium/Malarone/Artemisia were all developed in an attempt to kill the parasite or prevent infection. **(1 mark)** • Trials have produced a vaccine (RTS,S) which has now been recommended as being safe for use, as prevention is better than cure. **(1 mark)** • Measures taken to prevent people being bitten by the mosquito: Education programmes such as the WHO's "Roll Back Malaria" campaign. In particular educating people in the use of Insect repellents. **(1 mark)** • Covering the skin at dawn/dusk when mosquitoes are most active to reduce the chances of being bitten. **(1 mark)** • The increased use of insecticide-coated mosquito nets at night was an attempt to stop the mosquitoes from biting people and passing on the disease as people slept. **(1 mark)** *Possible comments on the effectiveness might include:* • Insecticides to kill the mosquito were effective at first however the mosquito became resistant to DDT and alternative insecticides are often too expensive for developing countries. **(1 mark)**

Question			General marking principle for this type of question	Max mark	Specific marking instructions for this question
					• Mosquito traps have been effective at a small scale, but mosquitoes breed so quickly that it is impossible to trap them all. **(1 mark)** • The BTI bacteria in coconuts is a cheap and environmentally friendly solution, with 2/3 coconuts clearing a typical pond of mosquito larvae for 45 days. **(1 mark)** • Draining stagnant ponds is impossible to be effective on a large-scale, especially in tropical climates where it can rain heavily most days. **(1 mark)** • Using mosquito nets at night/covering up exposed skin is effective as mosquitoes are often most active during dusk and dawn. **(1 mark)** • Drugs to kill the parasite once inside humans have been effective for a spell, but the parasite often adapts and becomes resistant — this is true even of the Artemisia-based drugs in SE Asia. **(1 mark)** • Anti-malarial drugs often have unpleasant side-effects so may prevent people from completing the whole course. **(1 mark)** • They are also expensive to research, develop and produce, making them often too expensive for people living in developing countries. **(1 mark)** • Scientists have trialled a vaccine on children across Africa and the early results from this are encouraging (a 56% drop in malaria after a year with children who had the vaccine, compared with those who did not). **(1 mark)** • Putting larvae-eating fish such as the muddy loach into ponds. As the fish breed, this has the added advantage for farmers who can eat some of the fish and add extra protein to their diet. **(1 mark)** Or any other valid point
9.	(a)		For 1 mark, candidates should give one detailed explanation, or a limited description/explanation of two factors. A maximum of 3 marks should be awarded for answers consisting entirely of limited descriptive points, with two such points required for one mark. Candidates should be credited for both positive and negative impacts.	6	*Possible answers might include:* • Sea level rises caused by an expansion of the sea as it becomes warmer and also by the melting of glaciers and ice caps in Greenland, Antarctica, etc. **(1 mark)** • Low-lying coastal areas, eg Bangladesh affected with large-scale displacement of people and loss of land for farming and destruction of property. **(1 mark)** • Climate change refugees from areas such as Tuvalu or the Maldives moving to higher ground or to other countries will exert more pressure on resources such as housing, water and power supplies. **(1 mark)** • More extreme and more variable weather, for example hurricanes due to increased sea temperatures. **(1 mark)** • Globally, an increase in precipitation, particularly in the winter in northern countries such as Scotland, but some areas like the USA Great Plains may experience drier conditions. **(1 mark)** • Increase in extent of tropical/vector borne diseases, eg yellow fever, as warmer areas expand. Possibly up to 40 million more in Africa being exposed to risk of contracting malaria. **(1 mark)**

Question			General marking principle for this type of question	Max mark	Specific marking instructions for this question
					• Longer growing seasons in many areas in northern Europe for example, increasing food production and range of crops being grown. **(1 mark)** • Impact on wildlife and natural habitats, eg extinction of at least 10% of land species and coral reefs suffer 80% bleaching. **(1 mark)** • Changes to ocean current circulation, eg in the Atlantic the thermohaline circulation starts to lose impact on north-western Europe, resulting in considerably colder winters. **(1 mark)** • Changes in atmospheric patterns linking to changes in the monsoon caused by El Nino and La Nina. **(1 mark)** • Increased risk of forest fires, for example in Australia and California due to change in surface temperatures and changes in rainfall patterns. **(1 mark)** • Milder winters producing less snowfall in Scotland, with Met Office predictions of 50% less snow by 2080 threatening the Scottish ski industry. **(1 mark)** Or any other valid point
	(b)		For 1 mark candidates should briefly describe a strategy and offer one evaluative point. Further developed/detailed evaluative comments should be awarded 1 mark each. A maximum of 2 marks should be awarded for answers consisting entirely of descriptive points with 2 such points required for 1 mark. Avoid giving marks for candidate comments which are the opposite/reverse of points already credited.	4	• The Thames Barrier has successfully protected London from flooding on numerous occasions and is predicted to provide protection from "one in a thousand year" flood events. **(1 mark)** • However, a second barrier may be needed to cope with flooding beyond 2070 and advance warning systems need to be further developed to advise Householders of the potential risks of flooding. **(1 mark)** • To manage the effects of drought during periods of extended rainfall, the UK has implemented hose-pipe bans but these are unpopular and difficult to enforce. **(1 mark)** • London has built a desalination plant, which is only intended to be used in periods of extreme drought due to the high operational costs. **(1 mark)** • Scotland is reducing greenhouse emissions by increasing energy production from renewables, which were meeting 50% of the demand by the end of 2014. **(1 mark)** • However, there is opposition to schemes such as wind farms because of their visual impact and effects on local wildlife, making it difficult to meet future targets on green energy supplies. **(1 mark)**
10.	(a)		Candidates should refer to both social and economic impacts for full credit, although markers should be aware that many impacts could be considered both social and economic. 1 mark should be awarded for each detailed point. A developed point may be a detailed explanation of an impact, or may be two less detailed impacts. A maximum of 3 marks should be awarded for answers consisting entirely of limited points, with two such points required for 1 mark.	4	*Possible answers might include:* • Many people are trapped in poverty because multinational companies want to manufacture their product for the cheapest price possible. **(1 mark)** • Many countries are unable to make a decent profit on the goods they sell because they are forced to pay tariffs to developed countries in trading blocs. **(1 mark)** • Government subsidies and grants in developed countries allow companies to sell products at a cheaper price than is possible in many developing countries – undercutting local farmers. **(1 mark)**

Question			General marking principle for this type of question	Max mark	Specific marking instructions for this question
					• Many children work instead of going to school, and this causes an illiterate population, with the consequent lack of opportunities. **(1 mark)** • Creates a self-perpetuating cycle of poverty where the next generation are unable to access well paid employment due to being illiterate. **(1 mark)** • The lack of well-paid jobs means many people live in shanty town type accommodation, with little access to safe electricity and sanitation etc. **(1 mark)** Or any other valid point
	(b)		For 1 mark, candidates should briefly describe a strategy and offer one evaluative point. Further developed/detailed evaluative comments should be awarded 1 mark each. A maximum of 3 marks should be awarded for answers consisting entirely of limited descriptive points (ie no evaluation), with two such points required for 1 mark or where answers are vague or overgeneralised.	6	*For the Caribbean Community and Common Market (CARICOM) answers may include:* • Removing customs duties between member states, means that even the smallest Caribbean countries have access to a regional market, reducing their costs. **(1 mark)** • Encouraging member countries to purchase raw materials from other CARICOM countries generates more trade and wealth. **(1 mark)** • Spreading the benefits of industrialisation and encouraging industries to locate in the smaller countries creates employment and raises GDP. **(1 mark)** • The creation of a single currency makes trade between Organisation of Eastern Caribbean States (OECS) countries much easier as money is not lost in transactions. **(1 mark)** • Trading alliances such as the EU can control the trade terms for the benefit of its members and make it difficult for non-members to compete on the same basis. **(1 mark)** • By setting up tariffs and import duties that they charge non-member countries, which protects employment and industries within the EU. **(1 mark)** • By introducing quotas, putting a limit on the amount of products that a Non-member country can sell, this protects vulnerable groups/industries. **(1 mark)** Or any other valid point
11.	(a)		No marks for describing the trends shown on the graph; candidates must account for the differences. Award 1 mark for each developed reason, or for two limited explanations.	5	• Most of the global economic growth is happening in developing countries such as China which requires lots of energy to construct infrastructure. **(1 mark)** • An increase in population growth leads to increased demands for electricity for lighting and appliances such as televisions. **(1 mark)** • Unlike in developed countries, much of the economic growth in developing countries is based on energy-hungry manufacturing industries. **(1 mark)** • In a global economy many of the manufactured products are sold to developed countries, and therefore need to be transported around the world. **(1 mark)** • Along with large increase in passenger air travel which has led to the construction of a large number of airport terminals and aeroplane use particularly in South East Asia. **(1 mark)**

Question			General marking principle for this type of question	Max mark	Specific marking instructions for this question
					• As people in developing countries become more prosperous, car ownership rates will also increase. **(1 mark)**
					Or any other valid point
	(b)		Award 1 mark for each developed point or for two undeveloped points. Candidates must discuss a renewable source of energy. No marks should be awarded for discussing non-renewable sources of energy. Credit any other valid responses.	5	*Possible answers for all renewable energy sources might include:* • Struggle to meet demand of energy at peak times such as early evening due to rise in use of home appliances for evening meals. **(1 mark)** • Output is variable and depends on the weather conditions. This means that there are times when more energy is available than is required, whilst at other times, turbines may be switched off due to over-production. **(1 mark)** • Often located in remote parts of a country which means electricity is lost in transferring to areas of higher demand/population. **(1 mark)** *For Hydroelectric power (HEP) other possible answers could include:* • Even countries like Norway with very high HEP potential have to import electricity from Sweden during drier months. **(1 mark)** • Run-of-the-river power stations rely on the flowing water of a river and when river is in spate potential power production is lost. **(1 mark)** • Conventional HEP stations dam the river to create capacity, however this floods large areas of land which have serious environmental consequences. **(1 mark)** • Turbines can be easily and cheaply added to existing dams / reservoirs allowing power to be generated from multipurpose dams, generating energy from pre-existing infrastructure. **(1 mark)** • Pump-storage dams effectively allow power to be stored, as water is pumped to an upper reservoir and times of low demand (price). This water can then be released at times of higher demand (price) where the water is stored in a lower reservoir for future use. **(1 mark)**

Section 4: Application of Geographical Skills

Question			General marking principle for this type of question	Max mark	Specific marking instructions for this question
12.	(a) (b)		Candidates should make reference to all sources, including the OS map to discuss the suitability of the site and the social, economic and environmental impacts of the housing development on the surrounding area. 1 mark should be awarded for each developed explanatory point. 1 mark should be awarded where candidates refer to the resource and offer a brief explanation of its significance (beyond the wording of the resource), or give a limited description/explanation of two factors. A maximum of 5 marks should be awarded for answers consisting entirely of limited descriptive points, with two such points required for 1 mark.	10	*Possible answers may include:* **Possible advantages of the location:** • The site is located close to a number of transport links such as the M5 to the east leading to Weston Super Mare -or- A38 to Bridgwater which will allow for commuting. **(1 mark)** • The location is also close to a railway station (322470) this may appeal to a wide range of home buyers who may not wish to rely on a car for transport. **(1 mark)** • The site is located on a large expanse of flat land and this combined with ease of access will lower construction costs. **(1 mark)** • The site may also appeal to families as it is within driving distance of Exmoor National Park which may offer leisure activities. **(1 mark)** • The site is also close to the Bridgwater Bay National Reserve which offers scenic walks (River Parrett Trail). **(1 mark)** • There will be an increase in demand for housing due to the employment opportunities created by new power station. **(1 mark)** **Possible disadvantages of the site:** • The site which has been chosen lies less than 10 metres above sea level, therefore this area may be at risk of flooding in heavy rainfall. **(1 mark)** • The area chosen is a floodplain and this may increase the cost of construction due to the need to build flood defences. **(1 mark)** • The building of this development may also increase the risk of flooding in surrounding areas as run off will increase from the development due to less infiltration. **(1 mark)** • The development lies between a railway and the A38 leading to possible air and noise pollution. **(1 mark)** • Some residents may be concerned about possible safety issues relating to transport of radioactive material or waste from the nearby power station. **(1 mark)** **Social impacts:** • The increase in houses will help relieve pressure on the local housing markets which may have a shortage as a result of people moving into the area due to construction of the power station. **(1 mark)** • The building of this development is also needed to relieve the pressure on housing as the population in the area has increased by 18,000 between 1991 and 2011. **(1 mark)**

Question	General marking principle for this type of question	Max mark	Specific marking instructions for this question
	(continued)		• With the building of the development to include leisure facilities this will benefit the town of Highbridge, this may also help further the appeal of the holiday park as a holiday destination (304482). **(1 mark)** • Residents of Alstone (314468) may be unhappy that this quiet rural way of life may be disturbed by a large new housing development on their doorstep. **(1 mark)** **Economic impacts:** • Construction companies will be attracted to this area creating a number of skilled jobs boosting the local economy. **(1 mark)** • More impermeable surfaces may lead to increased risk of flooding meaning a rise in insurance premiums. **(1 mark)** • Increased population may lead to improved trade income for local small businesses. **(1 mark)** **Environmental impacts:** • The building of this development may see an increase in traffic and congestion on roads not just during construction as the building of 300 new homes will increase the population of the area, leading to more noise and air pollution. **(1 mark)** • The possible need for flood defences may have an adverse consequence on nesting birds and aquatic wildlife in the surrounding area. **(1 mark)** • Increased flooding is likely due to the more impermeable tarmac surfaces increasing run-off. **(1 mark)**

Acknowledgements

Permission has been sought from all relevant copyright holders and Hodder Gibson is grateful for the use of the following:

Population Pyramids for Ghana 2013 and 2050, taken from the US Census Bureau. Public domain (2015 page 5);
Congestion levels in UK Cities, as identified by TomTom © TomTom International B.V. (2015 page 6);
Image © gary yin/Shutterstock.com (2015 page 7);
The table 'Development indicators for selected developing countries' taken from the Central Intelligence Agency website (https://www.cia.gov/library/publications/the-world-factbook/index.html). Public domain (2015 page 10);
Diagrams taken from National Park Service U.S. Department of the Interior (http://www.nps.gov/goga/learn/nature/images/Greenhouse-effect.jpg). Public domain (2015 page 11);
An extract from 'Lake District Management Plan — State of the Park Report 2005: Access and Recreation' © Lake District National Park Authority (2016 page 4);
The table 'Trade Patterns of Selected Countries' taken from the CIA World Fact Book 2013 (https://www.cia.gov/library/publications/the-world-factbook/index.html). Public domain (2016 page 12);
An extract © Sussex Wildlife Trust (2016 page 14);
Two images © Department of Transport. Contains public sector information licensed under the Open Government Licence v3.0 (https://www.nationalarchives.gov.uk/doc/open-government-licence/version/3/) (2016 page 15);
An extract from 'World Malaria Report 2015', Country-level trends in malaria incidence and mortality, page 14. Copyright 2015 WHO (2017 page 7);
A quote from the article 'Climate impacts "overwhelming" — UN' by Matt McGrath from http://www.bbc.co.uk/news/science-environment-26810559 © BBC (2017 page 8);
An extract © Yeovil Express (Newsquest) (2017 page 13);
Ordnance Survey maps © Crown Copyright 2016. Ordnance Survey 100047450.